Preaching and Teaching
the Psalms

Preaching and Teaching the Psalms

James L. Mays

EDITED BY

Patrick D. Miller

and

Gene M. Tucker

WESTMINSTER
JOHN KNOX PRESS
LOUISVILLE • KENTUCKY

Scripture quotations from the New Revised Standard Version of the Bible are copyright © 1989 by the Division of Christian Education of the National Council of the Churches of Christ in the U.S.A. and are used by permission.

Scripture quotations from the Revised Standard Version of the Bible are copyright © 1946, 1952, 1971, and 1973 by the Division of Christian Education of the National Council of the Churches of Christ in the U.S.A. and are used by permission.

Scripture quotations marked REB are from *The Revised English Bible*, © Oxford University Press and Cambridge University Press. Used by permission.

"Calvin's Commentary on the Psalms: The Preface as Introduction," first published in *John Calvin and the Church: A Prism of Reform*, edited by Timothy George, is copyright © 1990 by Westminster John Knox Press. Used by permission of Westminster John Knox Press.

"The God Who Reigns: The Book of Psalms," first published in *The Forgotten God: Perspectives in Biblical Theology*, edited by Andrew Das and Frank J. Matera, is copyright © 2002 by Westminster John Knox Press. Used by permission of Westminster John Knox Press.

"There the Blessing: An Exposition of Psalm 133," first published in *A God So Near: Essays on Old Testament Theology in Honor of Patrick D. Miller*, edited by Brent A. Strawn and Nancy Bowen (Winona Lake: Eisenbrauns, 2003), 79–90, is used here with permission of Eisenbrauns.

"The Self in the Psalms and the Image of God," first published in *God and Human Dignity*, edited by R. Kendall Soulen and Linda Woodhead (Grand Rapids: Wm. B. Eerdmans Co., 2006), is used here with the permission of Wm. B. Eerdmans Co.

"Maker of Heaven and Earth: Creation in the Psalms," first published in *God Who Creates: Essays in Honor of W. Sibley Towner*, edited by William P. Brown and Dean McBride Jr. (Wm. B. Eerdmans Co., 2000), 75–86, is used here with the permission of Wm. B. Eerdmans Co.

"The Question of Context in Psalm Interpretation," first published in *The Shape and Shaping of the Psalter*, edited by J. Clinton McCann (JSOT Supplement Series, 159; Sheffield Academic Press, 1993), 14–20, is used here with the permission of Morehouse Group.

"Past, Present, and Prospect in Psalm Study" by James L. Mays, first published in *Old Testament Interpretation Past, Present, and Future: Essays in Honor of Gene M. Tucker*, edited by James Luther Mays, David Petersen, and Kent Harold Richards (Nashville: Abingdon Press, 1995), 147–56, is used by permission.

"What Is a Human Being? Reflections on Psalm 8" is copyright © 1994 *Theology Today* 50 (1994): 511–20. Reprinted with the publisher's permission.

Book design by Sharon Adams
Cover design by Mark Abrams

First edition
Published by Westminster John Knox Press
Louisville, Kentucky

This book is printed on acid-free paper that meets the American National Standards Institute Z39.48 standard. ∞

PRINTED IN THE UNITED STATES OF AMERICA

06 07 08 09 10 11 12 13 14 15 — 10 9 8 7 6 5 4 3 2 1

Library of Congress Cataloging-in-Publication Data is on file at the Library of Congress, Washington, D.C.

ISBN-13: 978-0-664-23041-8

ISBN-10: 0-664-23041-5

Contents

Preaching the Psalms

Editors' Foreword

Born into a family who were devout members of the Associate Reformed Presbyterian Church, a truly psalm-singing denomination of Scottish background, James Mays has prayed and sung the psalms all his life. For over fifty years he has also studied, taught, preached, and written extensively about the psalms. His commentary on the psalms in the Interpretation series continues to be the most all-around useful commentary on the psalms in English. Its scholarly acumen and its theological depth make it an interpretation of the psalms that is, at least for now, without equal in the midst of a large store of psalms commentary.

The commentary, however, which was published near the end of Mays's teaching career, is only part of the long and rich history of his interpretive work on the psalms. He taught the psalms to hundreds of students at Union Theological Seminary—PSCE in Virginia. Throughout all those years, he preached often on the psalms at Union and in various congregations. He often lectured both in academic contexts as well as to church congregations on the particular psalms and on the critical issues that confront anyone who seeks to delve deeply into their interpretation. Not surprisingly, when he presented his presidential address to the Society of Biblical Literature, he turned to the Psalter, taking up quite specific psalms but using them as a way of thinking about the shape and theology of the Psalter as a whole. That essay was published along with others Mays has written through the years in a collection titled *The Lord Reigns: A Theological Handbook to the Psalms* (Louisville, KY: Westminster John Knox Press, 1994).

As the present volume demonstrates, however, that collection only touched on the rich load of theological interpretation of the psalms that occupied James Mays right up to the present moment. For this reason we have gathered together a number of his pieces that have been published in journals or essay collections together with quite a few that have never appeared in print and offer them now to a wider audience. We presume that audience will comprise the academy, pastors, and lay folk, for they have been written for all of those audiences, and no one in any of those categories will find anything here that is not both understandable and helpful.

The first group of essays presented here are pieces that were written for a generally academic reader in some cases, such as the review of current study of the Psalms, and, in other cases—specifically the opening long discussion of "Psalms and Prayer"—for a nontechnical audience of Christian believers for whom the psalms are a basis for prayer and faith. Along with this large treatment of prayer in relation to the psalms, the rest of the essays treat major theological topics from the perspective of the psalms: Creation, anthropology, and the reign of God. In some of these, one will find virtually a small biblical theology, especially in the treatment of the human reality, a central concern of these essays as a whole, as one will see in turning to the expositions of Psalms 8 and 51, for example.

On the way to those expositions, however, Mays turns to two different concerns that have been important to him but also to the broader interpretation of the psalms. In his essay on the question of context, he takes up one of the dominant issues in contemporary psalms study: how do the varying contexts in which one reads a psalm—for example, the setting in life of the different genres, the context provided by the Psalter as a whole, and the context of each psalm in the whole of Scripture—affect one's hearing, interpretation, and appropriation of each psalm? In the last essay of this first section, Mays turns to one of the greatest of all the interpreters of the psalms, John Calvin. His essay focuses on Calvin's introduction to his commentary to learn from his work especially about the interpretive importance of the commentator and his readers. The essay illustrates the possibilities when presumably objective reading of the psalms is replaced by deeply pious and theological interpretation, one that is still firmly attentive to the text but always seeing it in the larger contexts mentioned above as well as in relation to the Christian community.

In the second part of this collection, Mays offers expositions of particular psalms. All of these are psalms that have played a large part in the church's use of the Psalter, whether in liturgy, preaching, or pastoral life and personal devotion. Some of these the reader may be sure Mays first learned—that means memorized—literally at his mother's knee. The expositions are richly theological and in some instances are matched by sermons on the same psalms offered in the final section.

It is not often that a scholar of Mays's renown for his work on a particular book of the Bible will expose himself also in the preaching of that book. Happily, this collection leads finally in exactly that direction. Those who have used his commentary on the psalms, of course, will not be surprised. Again and again in the commentary, exposition of a psalm leads to an articulation that seems on its way to the preaching of the text. Here, in this volume, he goes all the way, and we hear this master interpreter preach the word, listening to and proclaiming the psalms in the light of the gospel, the whole of Scripture, and the human situation. That is finally what the psalms are all about. One is not likely to hear that more clearly and contagiously than in these powerful expositions and sermons.

—Patrick D. Miller and Gene M. Tucker

Studying the Psalms

1

Psalms and Prayer

Congregational Lectures on Prayer-Psalms as Lesson and Liturgy

The subject is "Psalms and Prayer"—psalms composed as prayers, psalms as biblical instruction about prayer, and the possibility that psalms might be our prayer. The emphasis is on psalms, because prayer as a subject on its own is too great a challenge for me. I would never have the courage to teach about prayer. Jesus could handle the disciples' question, "Lord, teach us to pray." We note that he did not respond with a lecture or give instruction about a theoretical understanding of prayer. Instead, he gave them a specific prayer to pray as disciples. Perhaps his answer is a precedent for turning to the specific prayers in the book of Psalms.

Prayer remains for me a great mystery. I do pray. I believe in prayer as an essential dimension of my faith in God. I cannot imagine trying to live life's journey without prayer. But I do not understand it in the sense that I can explain just how it works and answer the questions that thinking about prayer as an activity can provoke. How can it be that I, one little speck of consciousness in the vastness of the universe and in the unending flow of time, should claim the attention of the One who is the infinity and unity of all reality?

Once, some years ago, I resolved to study prayer and to master it as a subject of learning. In my personal library there is a shelf of the best books I could find on the subject, a remnant and reminder of the effort. But I gave up. No more research. Just pray. How does prayer work? I don't know. In the course of my study I read what some wise and devout people have written, and I have been helped. I have reflected on my own experience. At one time in my life, I prayed to be able to go to college. I was an adolescent during the depths of the Great Depression, and the opportunity in those days was an anxious uncertainty. Now that I have spent most of my life in schools of various kinds, with my gratitude I also wonder about the relation between those immature prayers

3

and what happened. What comes to you in life as apparent answers to prayer is itself a great mystery.

So the plan is for us to concentrate on some actual prayers and ask how these psalms guide our thinking about prayer—and lead us in prayer. If in the process we are led a bit deeper into the psalms, then we will, I think, have been helped with the mysterious subject of prayer.

There are good reasons for turning to psalms in a quest for help with prayer. We need only remind ourselves of the significant role that psalms have had in Christian history and life. A brief review of that significance can provide a kind of justification for our strategy and open up some of its dimensions.

First of all, there is the obvious fact that the psalms are in the Bible. That the psalms are biblical texts may be obvious, but for traditions like ours that assign such a central place in our faith and life to the Scriptures, their biblical identity is important. It attributes a certain authority to them and leads us to approach them with an expectation of instruction and inspiration. There are many different kinds of literature in the Bible. Most are narrative in character, but there are also letters, collections of sayings from prophets and teachers of wisdom, and records of visions. Scattered through these various kinds of writings one comes on occasional prayers and hymns. But in the book of Psalms we have an anthology that places the activity of worship prominently in view as if to establish the canonical place of praising and praying. People in the narratives praise and pray, but the book of Psalms places these movements of faith themselves on the biblical agenda.

Second, there is the presence of psalms in the historic liturgy of synagogue and church. Jewish liturgies have always incorporated psalms in a prominent way. From its earliest beginning the church has employed the language and literature of psalmody as the stock of its worship. For most liturgical traditions within Christianity the practice has been continuous and unbroken. Presbyterians have a rich heritage of singing metrical versions of psalms as hymns, a heritage we almost lost in the last century but now are recovering through an effort to restore psalms to their traditional place in our services. Moreover, psalms have had an influence beyond the use of specific psalms. Their vocabulary and motifs penetrate the language of all parts of services of worship. They are a kind of mother lode of expression for how Christians think and speak in communion with God. In their continuing presence in Christian worship the psalms have served as an orienting norm for the material of common worship.

Third, the psalms have been the basic material Christians have used as individuals in the cultivation of their spiritual life. They have served as readings for contemplation and meditation as well as prayers that believers appropriate as their own. The voice of the psalmist became the voice of those who prayed through and with them. The story of the Christian movement, from Augustine to Bonhoeffer, is replete with the testimonies of those who found in the psalmic prayers the language for their own souls. Every guide and resource for Christian devotional practice is likely to feature psalms as a major component.

Finally, the psalms serve as an integrating and unifying factor for the life of faith. The Holy Scripture, congregational worship, and private prayer are all means of grace, vitally important for the progress of every pilgrim through the country of their own biography. Because the psalms are present in each they connect and relate these three foci of Christian existence. In fact all three are crafted into the form and content of the psalms. The book contains both individual prayers and congregational hymns arranged and ordered in an anthology that itself is designed to serve as Scripture.

In the classical practice of Christianity and Judaism, the entire book with all its psalms has been used as prayer. In liturgical and devotional use, all the psalms have been read, sung, and meditated on as prayer—prayers of praise, thanksgiving, trust, and reflection. The psalms in their variety contain examples suitable for all these various intentions and functions of prayer.

But it is the psalms written specifically as the petition of an individual on which I want to focus. These are the ones composed specifically as prayer. There are more of them in the Psalter than any other kind. By their number and intensity they have given color to the Psalter as a whole. They are precisely the psalms that have played a central role in the classical use of the psalms as prayer. If we are going to pray the psalms as our prayers, it is this group of psalms that we must engage.

The bad news is that they are the most difficult of all for contemporary Christians to own.

The good news is that their profoundest value lies in the problems, challenges, and provocations that they offer to our religious sensibilities.

The difficulties for most contemporary Christians in using the prayers in the Psalter as their prayers are plain to see. These difficulties are well illustrated in the very first of these prayer-psalms to appear in the book of Psalms, Psalm 3 (RSV).

> O LORD, how many are my foes!
> Many are rising against me;
> many are saying of me,
> there is no help for him in God.
>
> But thou, O LORD, art a shield about me,
> my glory, and the lifter of my head.
> I cry aloud to the LORD,
> And he answers me from his holy hill.

I lie down and sleep;
I wake again, for the LORD sustains me.
I am not afraid of ten thousands of people
who have set themselves against me round about.

Arise, O LORD!
Deliver me, O my God!
For thou dost smite all my enemies on the cheek,
thou dost break the teeth of the wicked.

Deliverance belongs to the LORD;
Thy blessing be upon thy people!

First, as is apparent from the arrangement of the sentences in the psalm, this prayer—as all the prayers—is a poem. The prayers are composed in balancing rhythmic sentences and phrases in order to give a musical quality to their rhetoric. They constantly employ metaphors and similes to convey meaning by stimulating and provoking the imagination. The vocabulary is often symbolic and elusive. The human condition is depicted in language that is typical, open, and evocative. The prayers communicate with the reader by prompting associations and stirring emotions and inviting reflection. One needs to linger here and dwell a while.

But poetry departed from American culture and education over two generations ago. Because of our loss of poetry as a common cultural possession, we tend to be doggedly literal and literalistic, accustomed to facts and figures and physical explanations. Time is compressed in our consciousness; we are hurried and impatient and trained by television advertising to expect the immediate message. This all leaves the question: can the poetic pray for us?

Second, the person in these prayer-psalms approaches and addresses God in a way that makes many uneasy. The one who prays seems not to have learned the etiquette of prayer to which we are accustomed. The qualities of reverence, deference, patience, and submission seem to be missing. Instead, these prayers have a pleading, passionate, insistent tone. They bring the one who prays them into close quarters with God, too close for comfort. Their language takes the form of a struggle with God, a Jacob-like wrestling that tries to grasp and hold on to God. They are not exercises in equanimity, articulations of selfless piety. To many of us they will seem to lack the manners of proper reverence.

Third, there appears to be a disparity between the need of the one who prays in the psalm and the circumstances in which we ordinarily find ourselves. The trouble described in the psalm is always ultimate; that is, life and status are at risk. Without God's help all is lost. From psalm to psalm the troubles are described in such plastic language that one cannot say just what specifically the trouble is, but the language leaves no doubt that the situation is extreme.

This urgency does not seem to match the course and conditions of our daily life. The strain and stress of our familiar routine may be bad enough at times, but we do not ordinarily experience life as a crisis. So we may be inclined to set these prayers aside, to reserve them for times when the bottom drops out, when we are in deep waters, for circumstances that appear to be like the ones described in the psalm. They do not seem suited for daily prayer, for devotions in the ordinary round of life.

Fourth, there is a distinction between the identity of the psalmist and my identity that hinders my owning the prayer. It is his, not mine, and I tend to be always conscious of the otherness of the person in the psalm. The psalmist is mostly said, in an introductory sentence, to be David or some other biblical character. The writers lived in the ancient world, a radically different culture.

Do I protest too much? This rehearsal of difficulties may sound like a litany of discouragement, when what is needed is encouragement to possess the riches of this poetic prayer. But there is a lesson here, an important lesson.

Currently, in religious publications and programs there is quite a bit of enthusiastic promotion of psalms, implying that all one has to do is take a psalm and start praying it. Perhaps one ought to try. But any facile, easy, superficial turn to psalm-prayer may well result at best in a rote superficiality, or at worst in discouragement.

It is better, I am persuaded, to have the problems clear as part of the process—to know, if one is a beginner, that you have to learn your way. Psalm-prayers are first of all Scripture. They require our patience and seriousness in their otherness. In getting to know their otherness we begin to know ourselves in a new way. As we seek to speak with the psalm we find ourselves speaking to God in a way only the psalms make possible. The psalm instructs us, "Repeat after me," and in that expectant repetition, psalmic prayer begins to happen for us.

Obviously, we cannot look at all the many psalmic prayers. Nor would the exposition of several achieve an adequate consideration of the character of the collection. So I propose to take as the agenda of our reflection the elements that are typical of all of them, the parts of which they are generically composed. Taking instruction from what is typical of them gives us some purchase on all of them, and I endeavor to draw on the actuality of the texts to keep the typical elements from becoming empty generalities.

One psalm in particular displays in such clarity and brevity the typical elements of which all are composed that it can serve as a paradigm and master illustration. It is the thirteenth psalm. As you read the following analysis of the psalm you can identify the typical parts of which these prayer-psalms are composed.

The psalm begins with a *vocative*, "O Lord." The one to whom the prayer is addressed is named; the addressee is called by name.

Then comes a *description of trouble*. These prayers typically speak of the trouble that is the occasion of the prayer in terms of the psalmist's relationship to God, to self, and to others. So the description is composed in terms of reference to the "Thou" of God and to the "I" of self and to the "They" of others. In Psalm 13 the first is: "How long, O LORD? Wilt thou forget me for ever? / How long wilt thou hide thy face from me?" In the second, the reference to self is: "How long must I bear pain in my soul, / and have sorrow in my heart all the day?" The third element, the reference to others, is: "How long shall my enemy be exalted over me?"

The *petition* typically has two dimensions. The first is a petition to be heard and the second a petition to be helped. Here the two are combined in the line "Consider and answer me, O LORD my God! / Lighten my eyes."

The petition is frequently supported by the statement of a *motive*, which as here is frequently attached directly to the petition. The motive that supports the prayer in Psalm 13 is, "lest I sleep the sleep of death; / lest my enemy say, 'I have prevailed over him'; / lest my foes rejoice because I am shaken."

The prayers usually include toward the end an *affirmation of trust*, here asserted in the poetic line: "But I have trusted in thy steadfast love; / my heart shall rejoice in thy salvation."

These prayers typically conclude by moving from the rhetoric of prayer to that of praise, as illustrated by the final line: "I will sing to the LORD, / because he has dealt bountifully with me."

THE VOCATIVE

The place of the vocative in the prayer-psalms teaches us, first of all, that prayer begins with the name of God. In fact, the designation for prayer in the Psalms is "to call on the name of the Lord." At the beginning there is always this vocative, this word of address. Prayer cannot begin without this identification, this evocation, this recognition of the one spoken to. In a profound sense, the entire essence of prayer is contained in the name spoken. In times of great stress and consternation of soul the believer may lack the words to compose a prayer and can only say the one word of the name (Lord, God), yet in the simple utterance of the name, prayer is made. The believer has called on the name of the Lord.

The name has this weight and power in part because of its complex levels of meaning. Remember that when "LORD" is used in the Psalms and generally in the Old Testament as the name of God, it is printed in capital letters to let the reader know that it is a translation of a combination possible only in Hebrew. It contains the consonants of the personal name of Israel's God (YHWH) and the vowels of the title "lord," the Hebrew word *'adonay*, so the name has a double effect. It identifies and recognizes the One to whom prayer is spoken, doing what a name at the beginning of speech to another does. The name as vocative makes it possible to say "you" to God; it is the clarifying antecedent for every pronoun and imperative used in prayer. But the name not only says "who" God is; it also declares "what" God is in relation to the one who prays. He is lord, sovereign, the one in whose power one's life is lived. The name alone is a way of saying, "Thine is the kingdom and the power and the glory." So the name as the beginning of prayer is foundational to prayer in important ways.

First, the name insists that the prayer is address. It is spoken to the one named. The actuality of prayer depends on the reality of the other. It is not merely conversation with the self or communion with the self, except as these happen in the presence of the Lord. God is there for me, known to me, listening to me. All this is actualized in calling on the name.

There are clues in the psalm-prayers that they were composed to be said out loud as a way to heighten the enactment of real address to another. "With my voice I cried to the LORD," says the psalmist. There is a lot of experience behind the claim that the psalm-prayers read aloud achieve a higher level of involvement. Words spoken rather than just read silently involve the whole consciousness more completely. Saying prayer aloud lends a heightened sense of reality to the self at prayer.

The name as the beginning of prayer is a critical indication of the meaning of prayer. This act of a human being addressing another and speaking to that other personally, when there is nothing like what is usually known as a person there to listen—this is an astonishing act. It has rightly been called the supreme enactment of faith. When I pray the psalm I say to the mystery of the universe and to the mystery of my own existence, "Lord." Why is the world and what does it mean? How did I come to be, to be me? Why does my life take this course? When I pray the psalm, I name the inexplicable and speak directly as if to a person, to the power behind and in all the impersonal powers of world and life.

The psalm-prayers can speak to the eternal, person to person, because the name has been filled with a knowing that is like the way persons come to be known, except for sight and appearance. We otherwise know persons by what they do and what we experience with them and the character they thereby assume in our memory. "Oh, you know Frank Smith," we say. "He's the fellow we went fishing with last fall who dropped the whole stringer of fish over the side." "Now I know who you are talking about," we respond.

That is a trivial illustration, but by holy analogy the name "LORD" is like that. It contains a store of memory, stories all connected into one big story that runs from Abraham through David and Isaiah to a climax in Jesus of Nazareth and reaches on through the tribulations and triumphs of the church's history to the lives of parents and friends, and to us. The name has all the potential of that knowing memory when it is spoken into the void of the universe in the loneliness of human existence. By it the unknown becomes there for us in the person of the Lord.

Moreover, it is in this vocative that the psalmist and we who pray the psalm are given our identity. In the vocabulary of Scripture, whoever calls another "lord" is that one's servant. In the biblical literature "servant" simply means one whose identity and doing is defined by a relation to another. In some of the prayers the psalmist will say to another, "I am your servant." But whether this acknowledgment is present in the text of the psalm, it is always implicit in the pronunciation of God's personal name as "LORD."

So in calling on the name of the Lord we are also saying something about ourselves: "I belong to you. Through creation and covenant and Christ and Church I belong to you. I am not my own and I cannot make it on my own, no matter how fiercely I may seek to be independent and to run my own life. No matter how bravely I may rehearse my declaration of independence: 'I am the master of my fate; I am the captain of my soul.' The truth is that I am limited and dependent. I did not order my birth, nor do I command my death. In life I am vulnerable to powers I do not control." In his well-known hymn George Matheson got it right when he wrote:

> I sink in life's alarms
> When by myself I stand.
> Imprison me within thy arms
> And strong shall be my hand.

The human soul is free only when it is captive to the Lord. So the psalms teach us to begin praying with the divine name.

DESCRIPTION OF THE TROUBLE

After the vocative comes the description of trouble. These prayer-psalms are all prayers of persons in need of help. Every part of the prayer refers to, or at least assumes, the trouble and distress that occasions the prayer. But there is always one part that itself describes the trouble, one part where the psalmist tells the Lord about the hurt, need, and loneliness that drive the prayer. These tellings are often the most intense and poignant areas of the prayers. That, of course, is no surprise, because here pain seizes words and translates agony into speech—speech that conveys and holds need up to God. These words convey an almost childlike telling God what hurts, except the hurts are the kind that wound the soul.

In spite of the emotional quality of these descriptions of trouble they are not disordered, inchoate tellings. They follow a threefold pattern that is a kind of paradigm of the dimensions of human existence. They are based in an understanding of what constitutes human life and employ a vocabulary that was created in the realities of experience.

The troubles described in the prayers always in some way involve the loss of what in Hebrew is called *shalom*. The word is familiar. It has almost passed in our English vocabulary in some circles into a term meaning "peace" in a broad sense. In its own religious world *shalom* is a comprehensive term for a condition of life, a quality of experience, a state of being. A person has *shalom* when life is whole, when one is experiencing the wholeness that makes life complete. It is the health and well-being of living in all its levels. The apostle Paul speaks often of this wholeness in sentences like, "May the God of Peace himself sanctify you wholly; and may your spirit and soul and body be kept sound and blameless at the coming of our Lord Jesus Christ" (1 Thess. 5:23).

In the dimensions of wholeness, the completeness of life, the pattern of describing troubles is based. *Shalom* is constituted and experienced in relation to self and others and God. *Shalom* is present where body and mind are well, where the relation to others is positive, and where the presence of God is sensed and felt. That is precisely the threefold pattern of trouble lamented in the psalms. To use categories of classification, the trouble is personal, social, and theological. The psalmist is afflicted in body or mind or both. He is lonely, isolated, opposed, threatened by others. The goodness and health of God is not experienced, so God is felt to be absent. This is the agenda of need in the prayer-psalms. Either one or two or all of the three are iterated. Guided by this pattern the prayer-psalms tell the trouble to God. These are not "bite your tongue and bear it" prayers. Here pain and alienation and isolation are given their voice.

This threefold agenda of trouble and the vocabulary with which it is spoken are the features that make the ancient poetry so open and available to folk in every age. People find themselves in the prayers and come upon words that fit their feelings. We read, and suddenly there is a phrase, a sentence, we recognize a resonance, then read again as if hearing the words said about us, to us, for us.

John Calvin said of these prayer-psalms, "Here the Holy Spirit has represented to life all the griefs, sorrows, fears, doubts, hopes, cares, anxieties, in short, all the stormy emotions by which human minds are wont to be agitated." Believers across the ages have found this true of the psalms. The descriptions of trouble furnish a kind of glossary of distress complete enough to account for the whole range of human afflictions. It is often not possible to translate physical pain or anxiety or rejection into words that say what is happening in us and to us. The prayer-psalms translate for us. They translate inarticulate afflictions into the language of faith and bring it into the presence of God.

The importance of the descriptions of trouble in the prayer-psalms does not mean that these prayers are useful only as a liturgy of our distress. They speak not only for us, but to us as well. When psalms are used in a regular way as part of spiritual discipline, as they ought to be, they have the power to disclose us to ourselves. We not only find ourselves in the prayer-psalms; the prayer-psalms find us out. A divine who lived with them once called them "a vast step in the revealing of man to man."

In the round of regular reading, the threefold description of trouble can become a kind of diagnostic probe, an insistent counselor who holds up before me the mirror of mortality. The prayer-psalms are the poetry of the human condition, composed on the basic structures of human existence. Their telling of affliction speaks of bodies and psyches, of fabrics of relations to others and of a vulnerability to transcendence. This is the human condition—to exist as a physical and mental entity set in a skein of relationships to other humans and haunted by a sense of the divine. This poetry portrays the human condition in its finitude and fallibility, in its limitedness and sinfulness, in its mortality. We want to live and we are dying. We want to be in control of our lives, but life happens to us. We want to be known and loved by others, but we are unknown and in our hearts alone. We need the justification of our existence, but we are questioned and ignored. We want to know the answers and understand the mystery of life, but all we know is a riddle and we are left with enigmas.

As we read and ponder this poetry of the human condition, it can ask us, "What about you? Do you know yourself? Do these voices of pain and alienation and dereliction have anything to do with you?" When one begins to engage the psalms in a profound way, it can come to seem as if the psalms are reading and writing us. They are, these voices, a school in the neediness that belongs to the human condition, and that is important because these prayer-psalms would hold that you cannot truly pray unless you know your neediness.

Now with all that said, claimed, and affirmed, we must also recognize that elements of these descriptions of trouble make us uncomfortable. The concerns brought to God in prayer are here shaped in a way that does not seem to conform to our usual habits of prayer. For many, there are rough edges in the way the psalmists present their troubles to God in each item of the threefold agenda and, one must add, even in the practice itself.

To begin with the latter, there is a very strong tradition in Christian piety that views any lament or complaint or crying out to God as a failure of faith.

- In relation to God: It is more the practice to describe ourselves in prayer as beneficiaries of God's love and grace rather than as suffering from his absence or anger.
- In relation to self: We are accustomed to present ourselves to God primarily as sinful rather than urging the afflictions of our mortality.

- In relation to others: The frequent reference to enemies featured in these descriptions of trouble runs counter to our religious mandate to love others and our cultural ethic of accepting others.

I will reserve the second (addressing God as absent or angry) and the third (the emphasis on our finitude rather than our failures) until we are looking in a more comprehensive way at what happens with these prayer-psalms as we situate them in Christian piety.

About the first, whether lament and complaint is a failure of faith, there seem to be two rather different attitudes in the Christian tradition. The contrasting convictions on the question can be illustrated by quotations from hymns that are all included in the hymnal in current use in most Presbyterian churches.

First, here are some hymnic lines that seem to deny lament about the troubles of life a positive place in piety.

> Lord, I would place my hand in thine,
> Nor ever murmur or repine;
> Content, whatever lot I see,
> Since tis my God that leadeth me. (Joseph Gilmore)

> What can these anxious cares avail thee,
> These never ceasing moans and sighs?
> What can it help, if thou bewail thee,
> O'er each dark moment as it flies?
> Our cross and trials do but press
> The heavier for our bitterness.

> Only be still and wait God's leisure
> In cheerful hope, with heart content
> To take what e'er thy keepers pleasure
> And all discerning love hath sent.
> Nor doubt our inmost wants are known
> To Him who chose us for his own. (Georg Neumark)

> And when this cup you give is filled to brimming
> With bitter suffering, hard to understand,
> We take it thankfully and without trembling
> Out of so good and so beloved a hand. (Dietrich Bonhoeffer)

And, on the other hand, here are some stanzas that seem to encourage us to make our troubles the content of prayers to God.

> Jesus, lover of my soul,
> Let me to they bosom fly,
> While the nearer waters roll,

While the tempest still is high;
Hide me, O my Savior, hide,
Till the storm of life is past;
Safe into thy haven guide;
O receive my soul at last. (John Wesley)

What a friend we have in Jesus,
All our sins and griefs to bear!
What a privilege to carry
Everything to God in prayer!
O what peace we often forfeit,
O what needless pain we bear,
All because we do not carry
Everything to God in prayer! (Joseph Scriven)

Precious Lord, take my hand,
Lead me on, help me stand;
I am tired, I am weak, I am worn;
Through the storm, through the night,
Lead me on to the light;
Take my hand, precious Lord, lead me home. (Thomas Dorsey)

The contrast between the two sets of quotations is apparent. On the face of it, there appear to be two opinions about making our troubles the content of our prayers. I think I was reared and raised under the influence of one more than the other. I do not attempt here to adjudicate between them. Both have a strong presence in the Christian consciousness. Is "Only be still and wait . . ." ultimately contradictory to "carry everything to God in prayer"? I suspect that in the long last they are two sides of the same truth, another example of the way prayer comprehends opposites.

The question set by the pervasive presence of "enemies" in the catalogue of troubles that beset the psalmist is a more complicated one. Remember that the very first of the prayer-psalms in the book, Psalm 3, begins, "O LORD, how many are my foes! Many are rising against me," and in the following psalms the hostile forces are regularly there. As long as we are reading a psalm-prayer as Scripture, enemies that afflict the psalmist can simply be considered part of the narrative past. We may be astonished that the hostile people were so frequently a factor that occasioned prayer in the Old Testament world, but we can assume that the historical and social world of the book of Psalms was quite different from ours. John Calvin once observed that the story of David in the books of Samuel shows that David had enough enemies to account for all those we hear about in the psalms.

When the psalms are used as congregational and personal prayer the enemies become more of a problem, first of all because they are so frequently there as part of the problem prayed about. We would, I think, prefer to believe that we do not live in such a conflicted world. Then, in a few of the psalm-prayers, the ones usually called "imprecatory psalms," the psalmist prays not just to be delivered from the enemies, but also that God curse and obliterate them as a way of deliverance. I will save this specialized question of prayers against the enemy until we consider the effect of Christ on praying the psalms.

As we consider what to make of this more general problem, it is important to take a focused look at what is actually going on in these prayers.

1. The enemies are designated by general undefined terms and are never specifically identified or named. They are called enemies, foes, workers of evil, the wicked, pursuers, adversaries, and so on. Their actuality is constituted simply by the fact and character of their role in the predicament of the psalmist. The language used to refer to them is multivalent and open and appears to be a way of characterizing the experience of being beset and opposed and threatened.

2. The figure of the enemy turns up even in a context in which a personal enemy seems unlikely and inappropriate. For instance, in Psalm 6, which is a prayer of a person who obviously is suffering a physical affliction, the enemy nonetheless appears. One has the impression that there is a convention or tradition about the composition of these prayers for help that almost requires a reference to hostile forces. The "enemy" seems to belong to the formal and typical genre of describing trouble and symbolizes a way of thinking about "trouble and woe" in the cultural world of the psalmists.

3. What the enemies do is depicted in conventional and poetic imagery drawn primarily from the spheres of warfare, hunting and fishing, and wild animals. The sources of the imagery indicate that its function is to evoke the impression of attack, pursuit, and ferocity. This approach suggests that the enemies' activity is being depicted with the resources of metaphor and imagination rather than factual description.

4. The modes in which hostility is enacted are primarily verbal (slander, lying, insults, accusation) and relational (treachery, rejection, desertion, oppression). The capacity of evil to hurt is vested in personal agencies, and its target is the person.

5. The hostility of the enemy is given significance by using a pattern of opposites as its conceptual setting: servants of the Lord versus those who say there is no God; the righteous versus the wicked; the weak versus the strong. The use of these contrasting pairs to characterize the situation of hostility gives a moral and theological perspective to its experience.

6. The danger of the enemies is their threat to the psalmist's relation to God by subverting trust and hope, calling righteousness into question, and in general destroying the *shalom* willed by the Lord for the servant of the Lord. The

enemy in these prayers is the hostility to life and faith that puts in question one's relation to God.

When all the above are drawn into consideration of the problem of the enemy in the psalms, it is obvious that one cannot simplistically and directly identify any and every hostility encountered by the believer with the enemies in the psalms. In every case what is at stake in the encounter with the enemy is the psalmist's relationship to God. The threat and conflict is always theological.

Even so, there are implicit dangers in the way the constant reference to enemies in these prayers can work on the subjectivity of those who pray them. The prayers can become scriptural language for paranoia and putting the blame for one's problems on others, encouraging self-dramatization as victim. Because of such dangers these prayers have often been edited for use in liturgy in congregational worship and in personal devotions. The sections that deal with enemies are simply omitted. For instance, when the beautifully reflective Psalm 139 is used, verses 19–22 are left out, a procedure that should leave us uneasy about our violation of the structural character of these prayers.

Those who have pondered the psalms through the ages have learned that features of them that cause difficulty in use often turn out to be profoundly productive for understanding our life under God. The presence of all these metaphors of hostility and opposition in the prayers may be a way of keeping us aware that the way of faith is always a conflicted way, never completely at ease with the culture in which it lives or in agreement with the opinions and convictions that are derived from other sources than the way of the God of Israel and the life, death, and resurrection of Jesus Christ. One observer of American culture has said, "The true religions of America are optimism and denial." Middle-class and Protestant Americans tend to believe that evil can be conquered by being nice, or they take a hard line against whatever opposes them as if its simple opposition were enough to make it evil. One of the leading theologians of our time has argued that if the practice of Christianity does not provoke opposition and encounter enmity, it is not authentic Christianity. That may be worth some long, long thoughts in the context of pondering the context of the enemies in the Psalms.

PETITION

Next comes the petition, the asking for help that goes with the telling of trouble. The petition is the organizing element in the prayer-psalms. All the other elements prepare for the petition, as well as explicate and support it. The moment of asking is the climax, the pivot on which the whole turns. Wherever the petition comes in the composition of the prayer (at the beginning, in the middle, at the end), it is the essential part assumed by all the others.

The centrality of petition in the prayer-psalms has been the occasion for theologians such as Martin Luther and Karl Barth to claim that we have not prayed unless we ask. Prayer is not complete, not authentic prayer, until and unless God is asked. This concept is a severe challenge to many kinds and notions of prayer, but these theologians argue that we deceive ourselves if we speak to God in any other guise than that of the needy, in any other condition than that of neediness. Otherwise one would seem not to need anything from God, to be somehow sufficient before God. And if one is needy and will not ask, it is a failure of faith or a show of pride. "I am poor and needy," says the psalmist. The petition is the consummate expression of that neediness to God.

The petition in the prayer-psalms is typically twofold, a double request. "Hear me . . . help me" is the pattern. The two may come together or appear each at different points in the prayer, but these two modes of petition are interdependent, a pair, a paradigm of what is to be asked: hear me . . . help me. Each of the two has a simple set of synonyms used to express it.

> "Hear me" will be said, Rise up, O God: answer me; give ear; listen.
>   "Help me" will be said, Save me; lead me; heal me; vindicate me; guard me; do not be far from me; teach me.

This regular pairing indicates how closely the two requests are related. The psalmist cannot imagine God hearing without responding with help, and the pairing knows that to be heard is to be helped. It always helps to tell someone. The power of pain is diminished; the agony of anxiety is soothed when someone is told and hears. There is the catch: one must be heard. The saints of spiritual discipline tirelessly remind us that we must pray believing with all our hearts and knowing with all our trust that we are being heard.

The petitions in the prayer-psalms are not specific. You cannot tell from the typical way the petitions are expressed exactly how the psalmist expects the asking to be answered. The prayers do not lay out a plan of response and action that God is expected to follow. When the psalmist speaks of himself or his condition he can be expansive, but the petitions are more restrained and terse. "Hear me . . . help me" is what is asked. The prayers occupy ground between asking for particulars on the one hand and simply leaving it to God on the other. Surely there are times when prayer has to concentrate, to focus on one need. And certainly it is right for faith to say, "Thy will be done." It must, however, be remembered that these prayers are composed in the serious conviction that the Lord wills the *shalom* of those who belong to and depend on the Lord. Psalm 35 concludes with a declaration of this article of faith that is the foundation for all psalmic prayer: "Great is the LORD, who delights in the welfare [*shalom*] of his servant" (v. 27).

A friend who is an expert in the history of the Presbyterian Church in America tells me that the question of how to pray was one of the issues that divided the church in the early nineteenth century between the Old School and New School. The argument was over the asking in prayer. The New School people said, "Pray for rain or protection from the Indians or the conversion of a notorious drunk." The Old School contended that such prayer presumed to know the will of God, and they would pray only for general providence and for human concurrence with God's electing grace. It fascinates me that in those days how to pray was so serious a matter that the church would divide over it. Today we split over quite different, maybe less important questions.

Certainly the psalms do not authorize seeking God's attention to trivia. Lord, let there be an empty parking space at the shopping center. Lord, help Carolina make it to the Sugar Bowl. Kathleen Norris says that praying the psalms helps us learn how "to distinguish desires from needs." We live in a consumer culture that encourages an emphasis on our preferences and treats even whims as needs to be satisfied. This pandering to delusions of desire weakens the true self. The psalms clear our minds, let us know our true self by teaching us the distinction between what we want and what we need.

While the petitions do not deal in the particulars of desire, one would never call them vague or indefinite. The neediness voiced in the descriptions of trouble informs and expounds the help prayed for. These descriptions with their threefold options for naming the human condition allow those who pray the psalms to fill out the formulated telling of trouble with the specifics of their own life story. The petition becomes concrete as its language discerns and expresses the true neediness of our lives.

These prayers require a person to complete their meaning. Person and prayer go together. The person finds in the psalm the language to disclose the true self to God, and the psalm gains in the person the reality of the neediness of which its language speaks.

When you read and ponder these prayer-psalms, it becomes clearer and clearer that in all their asking what they seek is life—life not in the limited sense of biological existence, but life in the full sense that word can bear. Vitality of soul. Living that is fulfilled in the basic dimensions of human existence. Being vitally connected to self and others and God. The abundant life of which Jesus speaks in the Gospel of John.

In many of these prayers there is an explicit movement between life and death, and death, like life, is understood existentially. In the psalms death is not just what happens when life ends and we are no longer alive. Death invades life. The psalms speak of death as a dying that infects living. Whatever attacks or corrupts or weakens the soul's vitality is recognized as death, because it represents the power that negates life. Martin Luther wrote a hymn that says, "Even as we live each day, death our life embraces." He learned this profound spiritual truth from the prayer-psalms. When we practice praying by using them, they help us discern what truly threatens life. They teach us how always in our asking to seek life.

We can take the matter one step further and say that in expressing the neediness of life the petitions are asking for God. They do not so much ask God for something as ask for God. Their central and ultimate subject is the central and ultimate mystery of human existence—the incompleteness of the soul. In the psalms this is not the hidden agenda. It is talked about directly and in metaphors.

> "My soul thirsts for God, for the living God." (Ps. 42:2)
> "Whom have I in heaven but thee? And there is nothing upon earth that I desire besides thee" (Ps. 73:25)
> "O God, thou art my God; I seek thee, my soul thirsts for thee; my flesh faints for thee, as in a dry and weary land where no water is." (Ps. 63:1)
> "I say to the LORD. . . . I have no good apart from thee." (Ps. 16:2)

The answer the petitions seek is the self of God, the presence of God. "You have become my salvation," they say. Not just "You are my Savior," but "The LORD is my light and my salvation" (Ps. 27:1).

I found this unattributed quotation in John Bailey's *Diary of Private Prayer*: "He asks too much to whom God is not sufficient" (105). That sums up in a sentence the truth at the heart of the prayer-psalms.

THE MOTIVE

In the psalm-prayers there is a feature that is closely associated with the petition. The prayers are not content simply to ask. They typically go on to give reasons to God why the petition should be heard and answered. Clearly, the purpose of these reasons is to persuade God, to move the Lord to respond. In formal analysis these elements of the psalm-prayer are designated "motive clauses."

Frequently these motive clauses are attached to petitions as dependent clauses introduced by conjunctions such as "for," "lest," and "so that." Sometimes the clauses are freestanding sentences, and one has to decide on their role by their content and location in the psalm. But whatever their syntactic arrangement, this part of the prayer demands attention because of its apparent audacity. Imagine! This human project of giving the Eternal reasons as though the Sovereign of the universe were not sufficient unto himself.

We can begin to see the basis of the courage and confidence underlying this enterprise when we look at the reasons more closely. Arranged by content, the motivating clauses fall into three groups. Here are some brief examples of each to illustrate the categories, though it must be remembered that the examples cannot adequately represent the range and literary ingenuity found in this feature.

First, the motive clauses lay before God the neediness of the petitioner. In ways appropriate to the particular prayer they say, "I am poor and needy, so you should help me":

> "Be not far from me, for trouble is near and there is none to help." (Ps. 22:11)
> "Turn thou to me and be gracious to me; for I am lonely and afflicted." (Ps. 26:15)
> "Deliver me from my persecutors, for they are too strong for me!" (Ps. 142:6)

Second, the motive clauses appeal to the relation between the psalmist and God. The psalmist says to God, "I am your servant." In the vocabulary of the Old Testament a servant is one who belongs to another, who in turn is responsible for the servant. The reasons play on various aspects of that identifying obligating relationship.

> "Let me not be put to shame, O LORD, for I call on thee." (Ps. 31:17)
> "Lead me in thy truth, and teach me, for thou art the God of my salvation." (Ps. 25:5)
> "Preserve me, O God, for in thee I take refuge." (Ps. 16:1)

Third, the reasoning points to the character and conduct of God. The psalmist makes claims on the divine response based on the self of God. God should answer, "For his name's sake," to cite a frequently used expression. God should respond in accord with what God has revealed about himself.

> "Help me, O LORD my God! Save me according to thy steadfast love." (Ps. 109:26)
> "Hearken to the sound of my cry, my King and my God . . . for thou art not a God who delights in wickedness." (Ps. 5:2, 4)

On these three bases the motive clauses lay the foundations of supplicatory prayer: the condition of those who pray, their relationship to God, and the character of God.

When you look at the place of the motive clauses in the prayer-psalm as a whole, it appears that these topics repeat the substance of other parts of the prayer. The psalmist's condition is already held up to God in the description of trouble. The relationship to God is evoked in the vocatives that usually appear in the petition. The character of God is proclaimed in the praise that concludes the prayer. But these correspondences are not mere repetition or a failure of rhetoric. The parallel of the other parts of the prayer with the motive clauses shows us how much the purpose of the whole prayer is expressed in them. The prayer itself is a motive clause, a cry, a calling out, a plea.

Another analogy may be drawn here, an analogy to any and every authentic engagement between persons. The concerns of the self, the character of the other, and a relationship that makes it possible for concerns and character to interact—these are the essentials of personal engagement. The analogy reminds us that at its heart psalmic prayer (and can we say "all prayer") is a self seeking in relation to an other, the *shalom* of the self. By the intensity and eloquence with which they articulate engagement with the other, the psalm-prayers teach and help us to prayer that is truly an engagement of persons.

But there are problems working here. Obviously the assumption supporting the motive clauses is that God can be persuaded. God can be moved, affected by human appeal to do what God might otherwise not have done. The cautious and fastidious at praying will think that God will do his own will, so prayer should only be an act of submission of the self to the will of God. The piety in us may protest that prayer is really about changing us, not changing God. Our rational reservations will wonder at the problems set into motion by natural causes and the potential of particular petitions in a universal context. Surely persuading God is a somewhat naïve and primitive practice of prayer.

Perhaps such uneasy questions can keep us from glossing over the reality here. The prayer-psalms do seek to persuade, and they are not an exception in the biblical tradition; the two Hebrew terms for prayer are a testimony to that. One, *tephillah*, means laying out a case or constructing an argument for one. The other, *tehinnah*, means appealing for gracious treatment at the hands of another.

The instruction of Jesus is completely consistent with this view of prayer. "Ask, and it will be given you; seek, and you will find; knock, and it will be opened to you" (Luke 11:9). The connection between human initiative and divine response could not be expressed more succinctly. And there are the unforgettable parables of the widow who wears down the unjust judge with her persistence (Luke 18:1–8) and the man who at midnight by relentless asking forces a reluctant friend to get up and help him (Luke 11:5–8).

Do the hope and intent to persuade mean that the psalm-prayers are not prayers according to the will of God? Do they confront the divine will with an alien human will? The prayers are based instead on a conviction that what the petitions seek is indeed the purpose of God. A careful reading of the reasons given God shows that every one is a form of a statement about the self of God.

In Psalm 86 the psalmist laments, "O God, insolent men have risen up against me . . . and they do not set thee before them. But thou, O LORD, art a God merciful and gracious, slow to anger and abounding in steadfast love" (vv. 14–15). The wicked do not set God before them, but this is precisely what the prayers do. The prayers "set God before them" as reasons that God should hear their cry. The reasons invoke God to be God, are an argument that the character of the Lord should become conduct, and seek to move God to do the will of God on earth in the life and need of the psalmist.

The afflicted set before them the God who delivers the weak from those who are too strong for them (Ps. 35:10). The accused and rejected set before them the God who hears the cry of the righteous and turns aside the wicked (Ps. 5:4, 8, 11–12). The sinner sets before him the God with whom is forgiveness (Ps. 130:4). And all the psalmists at prayer set before them "the LORD who delights in the *shalom* of his servant" (Ps. 35:27).

It is a great mystery that in the commerce between the human and the divine, God should be set before God as an appeal to God. It means that there is a kind of epiphany in the human hunger, a form of God taking shape in anticipation and waiting. The mystery, then, would not be mere paradox but rather the kind of mystery of which the apostle speaks, the unfathomable will of God to be present with humankind.

The psalms do not offer us any theoretical justification for prayers of persuasion. Nor is there anywhere in Scripture an attempt to formulate an answer in a rational way to all the questions that can be raised about such prayer. If we need to establish in a systematic or philosophical fashion the possibility of persuading the Eternal, the Bible does not help us. What the psalm-prayers do offer us is help from quite another direction. How that help is given is illumined in the way Jesus answers the disciples' request "Teach us to pray" (Luke 11:1–4). He does not respond by producing a manual of prayer, a set of guidelines, an explanatory introduction. Instead he said, "When you pray, say . . . ," and gives them a prayer.

That is what the psalms provide, and have provided for Jews and Christians for two millennia: prayers of persuasion, words that ask and seek and knock. These psalms, as it were, turn aside our uncertain or skeptical questions and offer us prayers to say. And the answers that come are answers to prayer, the peace that transcends understanding to keep our hearts and minds in grace. Such answers do not satisfy the questions of reason, but they demote them to second place in our pilgrimage.

There is an ancient Latin proverb that epitomizes this experience: *Lex orandi lex credendi*, literally, the law of praying is the law of believing. What is said leads to what is believed. The genius of the proverb lies in its reversal of what we take to be the usual order of things. The usual order puts believing before speaking. You work out your faith and your theology and then express what can be truly believed in worship and prayer. Confessions of faith have authority over liturgy. That is true, and there is a truth here not to be subverted.

But there is dialectically this other truth that believing happens to us, comes to us in the practice of prayer and worship. As we say the psalms the words are gates through which the spirit shapes the mind that is in us. In the sphere of devotion and liturgy it is also true that faith follows speech; believing is enabled by language.

ASSERTION OF TRUST

The prayers for help typically include as a constitutive element sentences in which the psalmist speaks of his trust in God and his confidence in God's relation to him. These statements are in effect confessions of faith. They read like little Psalm 23s crafted into the structure of the prayer. Some illustrations from representative prayers display their character.

> Thou, O LORD, art a shield about me,
> my glory, and the lifter of my head. (Ps. 3:3)

> Behold, God is my helper;
> the Lord is the upholder of my life. (Ps. 54:4)

> I cry to thee, O LORD;
> I say, Thou art my refuge,
> my portion in the land of the living. (Ps. 142:5)

> The LORD has heard my supplication;
> the LORD accepts my prayer. (Ps. 6:9)

The location of these assertions of trust in particular prayers will vary; they may come at the end or in the middle, or be repeated at several places. But they are always there, as if what the psalmist says to God about God is essential to the act of prayer. Only twice in the prayers for help, Psalms 39 and 88, do these assertions appear to be absent. When one studies these two carefully, they seem to be the kind of exceptions that prove the rule. In fact, there are a number of prayers in which this one component of the prayers for help has taken over and become the whole (Pss. 4, 11, 16, 23, 56 and 62).

As the illustrative verses cited above show, a major theme of these assertions is the relation between the psalmist(s) and God. There is a confident declaration in one of the prayers that sums up all the assertions: "This I know, that God is for me" (Ps. 56:9). This declaration has a ring of finality about it as a disclosure of the basis on which all prayer is made. Its certain parallel is the rhetorical question with which the apostle Paul opposes his trust in the gospel to every contradictory experience and power: "If God is for us, who is against us?" The proper New Testament lection to read as commentary on the psalmic assertions of confidence in God is surely Romans 8:31–39. For the psalmist and for Paul the relation to God is not an independent claim based in the one who prays and hopes, but is a bond that has been initiated and established by God, and therefore is the most certain dimension of the life of the one who prays. Sometimes the assertions of trust are simply statements about God: what God is like and characteristically does and has done. In these cases the assertions verge on hymnic praise and seem to do what praise does. But even here the assumption in the praise is that the God who is glorified is "my God."

The presence of these assertions of trust in the prayers for help are instructive about the nature of these prayers, and even about the nature of prayer itself. First of all, the assertions remind us that these prayers as a whole are a quintessential enactment of trust. Indeed, if one can put the acts of faith in an order of priority, prayer itself would come first. To pray is the fundamental act of faith. For individuals and communities to recognize the reality of God by speaking directly to God and to put their present and future welfare in the hands of God is faith at its most real. These prayers are the voice of lives often in the very worst of circumstances in which everything argues against the reality of God and the hope of rescue. Their insistent claim in such circumstances upon God as the sure and only hope has been called "the supreme act of religion."

Second, the assertions of trust offer the context in which other elements of these prayers are to be read. The complaints about God's anger or absence are to be understood under their guidance. They provide a counterpart to the descriptions of trouble and state a contrast, an "on the other hand," to the desperation and need recited in the descriptions of trouble. They remind us that the God who is said to be absent is being addressed as present. The God who is experienced as angry is relied on as the God of loving-kindness. The assertions of trust are in fact an assertion of God against the negations of experience and the denials of the world.

Third, the unity of these assertions with the prayer as a whole is a warning against a possible misreading of the prayers. Because these assertions of trust often are located at the end of the prayer after the descriptions of trouble and the petitions, the prayers have often been interpreted as a movement from despair to faith. The one who prays begins in discouragement and hopelessness and moves through the therapeutic leading of the prayer to the faith stated at the conclusion. Such an interpretation mistakes their character and misreads the nature of faith. Flannery O'Connor once said, "You arrive at enough certainty to make your own way, but it is making it in darkness. Don't expect faith to clear things up for you." Psalm 23, the best-known and -loved expression of trust in the entire Psalter, reminds us that the life of faith is always a walk through a dark valley and hospitality at a table prepared in the presence of enemies. The assertions locate trust not after but in the very midst of the finitude and failure of human existence.

Finally, the assertions are a witness to something about faith itself: that faith is first of all trust, and only then belief. What we believe about God and God's way with the world is vitally important to our personal and corporate life. Yet what we believe is a matter of convictions formed as a response to tradition and experience. Because that is so, beliefs are vulnerable to the challenges of fallible thinking and the erosion of the miseries of life. But trust at its heart is personal, the effect of another person on me. And trust in God is God's personal effect on us as persons. These prayers show that such trust is so much a part of one's personal existence that it accompanies us through every affliction and alienation and failure that life encounters.

PRAISE

In the book of Psalms the praise of the Lord is usually expressed in the form of hymns. Praise has its own genre, its own literary form through which God is glorified. But praise is also a component of the prayer-psalms. In some it is nuanced in statements about God. In a good number praise occurs as a separate element. Most frequently there is at the conclusion of the psalm an anticipation or promise of praise that looks forward to a condition and time when the prayer has been answered. In some psalms praise is simply offered as a conclusion of the prayer. Here are some examples.

> "I will give to the LORD the thanks due to his righteousness,
> and I will sing praise to the name of the LORD, the Most High." (Ps. 7:17)

> "I will sing to the LORD,
> because he has dealt bountifully with me." (Ps. 13:6)

> "In the great congregation I will bless the LORD." (Ps. 26:12)

> "And now my head shall be lifted up
> above my enemies round about me;
> and I will offer in his tent
> sacrifices with shouts of joy;
> I will sing and make melody to the LORD." (Ps. 27:6)

The inclusion of praise in the prayers for help has an effect on the way the entire prayer is read and understood. First, it helps to center the prayer on the reality of God. Though addressed to the Lord, the prayer speaks of the psalmist's neediness, his petitions and pleas, and his trust. But in praise there is speech whose content is God and God's way with us. Then, as act and anticipation, praise is a form of commitment and a dedication of life. By the inclusion of praise the prayer becomes not only a plea of the self but as well an offering of the self. Also, as act and anticipation praise expands the consciousness of time to include the time of joy as well as the time of pain. One of the psalms says, "Weeping may tarry for the night, but joy comes with the morning" (Ps. 30:5). Praise remembers the morning while it is yet night.

The inclusion of praise as an element of prayers for help also indicates something about praise itself—how it is offered and understood. The movement from prayer to praise, the connection between sorrow and joy, affliction and exultation, is not a peculiarity of the prayer-psalm. The movement appears in the narrative structure of stories like Exodus and Jonah and in the elegant prophecies of Isaiah 40–55. The book of Psalms itself is arranged so that in its first parts the prayers of David are featured and then, as the book moves toward its conclusion, the exuberant hymns of praise become dominant.

It seems there is an inner relation between the moments of prayer and praise, between the situation of neediness and that of thanksgiving. If praise does not contain the memory of needs that have been met, hurt healed, sorrow comforted, loneliness visited, of life instead of death, then praise loses its theme and reality. There is an argument here that we need to use the Psalter in its entirety. We need to read through its prayers on the way to its hymns. There has been a tendency in the church's use of the Psalter to employ only or primarily the hymns, but if we go to the joyous hymns and the psalms of trust only and too quickly, we will never know the true power and purpose of the hymns.

Perhaps there is also an answer to one of the questions about the contents of the book of Psalms in the way it moves from prayer to praise. There are so many prayers for help, but so few songs of thanksgiving in which an individual expresses gratitude because his prayers have been answered. Among these few are some of the best-known psalms in the Psalter: Psalms 18, 30, 116, and 118. But there are so few of them compared to the many prayers. Why? Is this disparity in the contents of the Psalter evidence that so few prayers were answered? Could that really be the explanation? It seems to me far more likely that in the course of its collection and use of the psalms Israel came to believe that the corporate hymns of praise were the proper response to the prayers and expressed the right and true acknowledgment of gratitude for God's response. Once again, in this matter too the prayers are prologue to praise.

THE PRAYERS FOR HELP IN THE CHRISTIAN BIBLE

Finally, I offer some general and concluding observations about a hermeneutical reality that we have been noticing and attending at different points in various ways. The prayers for help are part of a book of the Old Testament. This canonical identity has two dialogically related implications for the way we read and use them.

First, because the prayers are in the Old Testament, they are part of our Bible. They are for us Holy Scripture with all that identity means in an unqualified way. They have Scripture's claim on our faith and life. Since the birth of the church Christians have studied these prayers to better know God and God's way with us, and have recited these prayers in devotions and corporate worship. The difficulties posed by their origin in Israel's worship of the Lord in historical times before the event of Jesus Christ do not compromise their identity as our Scripture.

Second, because the prayers are in the Old Testament, they will be read and understood in the context of the entire Christian Bible with its second part, the New Testament. The New Testament does not replace the Old. Instead, the New Testament extends the story in the Old of God and God's way with the world to its central climax in Jesus Christ. When we read and use the prayer-psalms, we do so as believers who are informed and guided by our knowledge of that fulfillment.

These two implications of the Old Testament location of the prayer-psalms stand in dialectical relationship. They should be held together in our reading and use of the prayers. In their dialectic they lead to a more complex and multivalent way of understanding and using the prayers, one that Christian practice at its best has always followed.

To suggest how the dialectic works, I consider here a brief list of features of the prayer-psalms as agenda for illustration. The consideration follows three moves. First (a), the theological character of the feature in the psalm as Old Testament Scripture will be identified. Then (b), the claim of the New Testament about that feature will be sought. Finally (c), a proposal will be made about how the two combine in reading the psalm as scriptural word and witness.

1. The prayer-psalms are addressed to a God known and named.
    a. In the psalms, prayer is addressed to the Lord (YHWH), the name of the "maker of heaven and earth" who has chosen Israel as his people and has redeemed and made covenant with them. God is known through his story with Israel. The Lord is the one and only God and the God of the psalmist; prayer is made to no other. Prayer takes place in a relationship created by the identity of God and the belonging of the psalmist to the people of God.
    b. In the New Testament, the basis is laid for Christian prayer to be made to God the Father (a title and name founded in the filial relation of Jesus to the God of Israel), and both the Son and the Holy Spirit participate in the engagement of prayer (Rom. 8:34; 7:25; Heb. 4:14; Rom. 8:26–27). Prayer takes on a trinitarian character. The one God is three whom the New Testament knows through the event of Jesus Christ and the experience of the Holy Spirit.

   c. The God who is called "Lord" in the Psalms and Jesus who is called "Lord" in the New Testament merge in the meaning of the name/title in the psalms. The creator of the universe who made Israel his people and the Father of Jesus Christ are one and the same. Christians read and pray the prayer-psalms instructed by this larger knowledge of the God to whom prayer is made.

2. The prayer-psalms are based on confidence in God.

   a. The psalmists call on the Lord as their God and king who will deliver his servants in their weakness and vindicate them in their innocence. In affliction of all kinds they experience the absence and anger of God. But they pray in confidence that the God who chose and delivered and made covenant with them as a people wills their salvation.

   b. In prayer in the New Testament there is no lament over the absence or anger of God, because God has revealed his love in the affliction and prosecution of his Son for their salvation. No human or cosmic power can separate us from that love. The event of salvation in Jesus Christ has trumped the present experiences of trouble.

   c. Between salvation inaugurated and finally realized, the miseries of life in body and community persist. The use of the psalms gives voice to the continuing reality of helpless and innocent affliction. The juxtaposition of the cry in trouble and the proclamation of trust in the psalms finds a new unity in the love of God in and through the union of Jesus Christ with our humanity and mortality.

3. The prayer-psalms hold up to God in a cry for help the entire range of human suffering.

   a. In the psalms, affliction is either simply there, or the work of wickedness of others, or the punishment of God. It is a suffering in faith, but always a dilemma from which a deliverance is sought.

   b. In the New Testament, and anticipated by a few Old Testament texts like Isaiah 53, the possibility of a suffering that serves the will of God, a suffering for the faith, appears. The purpose of God can be present in and through an affliction that is not relieved.

   c. The continuing use of the psalms as prayer is restraint against the dogmatic interpretation of suffering that attributes every and all trouble to the "will of God." God's purpose of *shalom* for his servants holds. The prayer of Christ, "If it be possible let this cup pass from me," allows us to pray the prayers for help, as long as we also pray "nevertheless, not as I will, but as you will."

4. The prayer-psalms are mostly supplications.

   a. The prayers in the psalms are appeals for help for the person or community that is praying. Intercessory prayer occurs in the Old Testament, and there are a few intercessory prayers in the book of Psalms, but individual and corporate supplications are the most numerous.

   b. The commitment of Jesus in his life and death to ministry to others turned prayer toward a ministry of love and solidarity with others, and intercessory prayer became prominent in the New Testament and practice of the church.

c. In Christian practice the individual prayer-psalms were often used as vicarious prayer and said on the behalf of and in solidarity with others. Christians as they read the psalms heard Jesus in his identity with their mortality praying the psalms for them. The psalms were also said on behalf of others who suffered, such as the martyrs. The emphasis of the New Testament on intercession nurtured a way of using supplication as intercession, while the prayer-psalms gave intercession a language adequate for the suffering of those for whom prayer was made.

5. In the prayer-psalms sin and sinfulness are statistically a minor theme.
   a. There are relatively few prayer-psalms in which the sin of the psalmist is the central problem. In the majority of the prayers it is the problems of human mortality and vulnerability that are laid before God.
   b. In the New Testament sinfulness is the central neediness of the human condition. Confession of sin becomes the theme of self-description in prayer.
   c. The prayer-psalms that can be read as confession of sin have constituted a favorite lectionary in Christian devotion and worship. The use of the entire Psalter has kept a place for the range of physical and public and social experiences that constitute human neediness.

6. Forgiveness, divine and human, is a minor theme in the prayer-psalms.
   a. God's forgiveness of human failure appears as redemptive in a few psalms. On the other hand, petitions to be delivered from enemies are common in the psalms, and some prayers invoke God's wrath and destruction against the enemies.
   b. According to the New Testament, Jesus is agent and provision of divine forgiveness in his practice and passion. Forgiveness is regarded as the primary divine redemptive action. The disciples of Jesus are taught to forgive their enemies.
   c. The use of the prayer-psalms teaches and expresses the reality that the life of faith is conflicted and that faithfulness is often opposed by personal and social forces. There are enemies of faithfulness. In early Christian prayer the enemies of the psalms are often understood to be sin, death, and the devil, the powers from which Christ redeems. Use of the prayer-psalms argues against a reduction of salvation to the forgiveness of sin.

2

Past and Present and Prospect in Psalm Study

The course of the study of the psalms can be read as a story of shifting concentrations on their various features in the search for the best answer to the question "What is a psalm?"

Critical interpretation in the course of its explorations has selected different aspects of the psalms as the central clue to the answer. The feature taken to be crucial has tended to organize the interpreter's approach and evaluate the relative significance of the various aspects.

The psalms confront the interpreter with an array of features. In the Hebrew Bible there are 150 psalms. All are composed according to the conventions of Hebrew poetry, which include using various rhetorical devices to achieve effect and unity. Many of them are introduced by superscriptions made up variously of classifications, including directions for performance and attribution to authors or patrons. The attributions are mostly to David and to guilds of singers associated with him by tradition, the Korahites and Asaphites. The psalms appear as the voice of an individual, others of a group; in some, both individual and corporate styles appear. Except for a few duplicates, each psalm presents distinct differences, yet continuities of vocabulary, themes, and arrangement run through many of them. Moreover, psalms refer to certain institutions of Israel's religious life: temple, king, sacrifice, processions, and pilgrimage. The book of Psalms is divided into five "books" by doxologies at the end of Psalms 41, 72, 89, and 106; beyond that there is no obvious arrangement of the collection except for the predominance of prayers toward the beginning and of hymns of praise toward the end.

THE BACKGROUND OF OUR CENTURY

Traditional interpretation took the attributions to David and his musicians as the decisive clue to the identity of the psalms. The psalms were read largely as the expression of the piety of David in the many situations of his life as narrated in the books of Samuel. Thirteen of the superscriptions refer to such situations, and these connections were taken to be paradigms for all the other psalms of David. For centuries the connections with David sponsored a rich and useful interpretation. The traditional approach did not think of David as a strictly historical figure. Rather, David was a paradigm and prototype in a canonical context. In the psalms he exemplified prayer, praise, and piety for Israel. He was the anointed king, the once and future messiah. The psalms as his prayer and praise provided instruction and prophecy. The best of traditional interpretation drew on the psalms for spiritual and theological purposes that enriched the life of Judaism and Christianity. The psalms' identity as Scripture controlled their identity as expressions of David's piety.

In the latter part of the nineteenth century, historical criticism called into question the Davidic identity of the psalms. Historical critics began to look at the incongruities between the details in many psalms attributed to David and the account of David's career in Samuel as well as at the connections between many psalms and biblical literature from times later than the period of David. The individual and corporate experiences described in the prayers and hymns were considered from a historical rather than from spiritual and theological perspectives. The psalms were regarded as the voice of some historical person or occasion. But lacking the occasion and/or person supplied by the Davidic connection, interpreters were left to search through the record of Israel for other plausible times and people as a context in which to read the Psalms. The tendency was generally to locate them later rather than earlier in Israel's religious history. The results of this venture were largely inconclusive, especially since the poetic language of the psalms supplied almost no details that could be linked with particular historical contexts. The psalms did not seem to be defined by the individuality and particularity of time, place, and event.

PSALM STUDY IN THE TWENTIETH CENTURY

Around 1900 form criticism emerged as a corrective to the historical approach to psalms. The preeminent figure in the shift was Hermann Gunkel. In his work he employed two principal concepts, *Gattung* (genre, type) and *Sitz im Leben* (setting-in-life, social context). Gunkel concentrated on the very features that had frustrated historical criticism; the general, formulaic, and repe-

titious character of the language in which the psalms are composed. Because
of these features he concluded that psalmic language is typical in reference
rather than historical; that is, it refers to types of persons and situations. The
psalms could be sorted out into categories of types, a limited list of genres, on
the basis of common vocabulary, themes, and arrangements. The various types
had emerged from and belonged to various occasions in Israel's religious practice. Each type derived from a setting-in-life, the verbal dimension of a religious performance. So the psalms were not texts rooted in unique historical
circumstances but instances of a genre that belonged to occasions that
occurred again and again in the course of Israel's religion.

The genres identified by Gunkel have provided a standard instrument for
the interpretation of psalms in this century. Refinements of his list have been
proposed, but hardly a work on psalms appeared in the twentieth century that
did not employ some version of Gunkel's types. The six major genres into
which he incorporated most psalms are these (the cited psalms are paradigmatic instances of the types):

1. Hymns, songs of praise for festival occasions (Ps. 100), including two smaller
   genres identified by particular themes: Songs of YHWH's enthronement
   (Ps. 47) and Songs of Zion (Ps. 48).
2. Laments of the Community, songs of appeal to YHWH in a time of
   national distress (Ps. 44).
3. Laments of the Individual, psalms of appeal by an individual in a time of
   personal distress (Ps. 13).
4. Thanksgiving Songs of the Individual, songs of witness and gratitude for
   answered prayer (Ps. 30).
5. Royal Psalms, psalms of various functions that belonged to ceremonies
   centering in the anointed king (Ps. 2).
6. Wisdom Poetry, psalms composed under the influence of the wisdom tradition, designed to instruct in piety (Ps. 37).

Besides these major genres, Gunkel created a list of minor genres to account
for formulaic features in some of the psalms and to account for the few beyond
his major genres.

For Gunkel's interpretation of psalms, the notion of genre was more important than setting-in-life. Through the genres derived from cultic practice,
many of the actual psalms were, in his opinion, "spiritual songs," personal
songs from the religious life of the pious individual. The truly cultic songs
were earlier, he thought, and the spiritual songs, later.

In contrast to Gunkel and his followers—for example, Claus Westermann—
other form critics have placed more emphasis on the importance of setting-in-
life for the interpretation of particular psalms. The most influential name here
is probably Sigmund Mowinckel. These critics have tended to identify most

psalms as agenda for performance in cultic ritual. They have searched the book of Psalms, other Old Testament books, and the literature of other peoples in the ancient Near East for evidences of festivals and ceremonies that might plausibly constitute the settings in which types of psalms were used. More psalms were judged to be early cultic pieces. The liturgy for festivals with themes such as the kingship of YHWH and Zion and covenant renewal was reconstructed as the setting for congregational psalms. A much greater role was assigned to the king as a major figure in the cult. Attempts were made to determine the specific problems referred to in the individual laments and to reconstruct the ceremonies in which they were used. Nevertheless, no general agreement has emerged that would determine the specific cultic setting-in-life of each psalm. Still, this effort—the cult-functional approach—has focused attention on the relation of psalmic literature to the religion of ancient Israel.

During the late nineteenth and throughout the twentieth centuries, an impressive body of literature from ancient Egypt, Sumer, Babylonia, and Assyria, the other national cultures contiguous to Israel, has been discovered and translated. The discoveries include hymns, prayers, royal literature, and wisdom texts, all of which have recognizable similarities to the psalms. This material has made it possible to view the canonical psalms as part of the religious literature of the ancient Near East. Similarities between the vocabulary, motifs, and elements of Israelite hymns and prayers and those of other national cultures provide confirmation of genres and their characteristics as features of a general religious culture. The poetic character and language, particularly in the texts from Ugarit, have been used to analyze and translate psalmic texts. Possible dependence of psalms like Psalms 29 and 19 on earlier texts has been explored. This collateral literature constitutes the primary source for data used in reconstructing cultic occasions and ceremonies as settings for Israel's psalms.

Psalm 3 can illustrate these diverse interpretive perspectives. Psalm 3 is introduced by a superscription identifying the psalm as a psalm of David when he fled from Absalom. The psalm is a prayer of an individual who laments the opposition of many enemies, professes trust in YHWH, appeals to YHWH for deliverance, and asks for blessing on the people of YHWH.

- The traditional approach would be guided by the superscription and point to the details in the psalm that correspond to features of the story in 2 Samuel 15. It might dwell on David's confident faith in the Lord in the face of insuperable odds and commend his concern for the people of the Lord in the midst of his personal trouble.
- The historical-critical approach might seek a context in the Maccabean period and attribute the psalm to a leader caught in the partisan battles and struggles of that time.

- The form-critical approach could view the military language in the psalm as metaphorical and interpret the psalm as a prayer composed for an individual in some indefinite but overwhelming trouble.
- Those who emphasize the importance of cult might conclude that Psalm 3 was composed for use by a king of Judah in ceremonies during which he professed his dependence on Israel's God, using the reference to many enemies as hyperbole to enhance his profession.

In all these instances, a general hypothesis about the character of the psalms affects decisively its interpretation. (The interpretations listed above report the conclusions of representative scholars but do not exhaust the possibilities of a particular approach and are given only for heuristic purposes.)

Though they are employed in different ways by different scholars who reach quite varying conclusions, the concepts of genre and setting-in-life and the body of literature comparable to the psalms from the ancient Near East are important features of contemporary psalm interpretation. They are certain to play a role, however qualified, in the future study of the psalms. But there is a growing dissatisfaction with these approaches. Among the important difficulties are these:

- Many psalms do not correspond exactly to the standard profiles of the genres to which they are assigned. They include extra elements that go beyond the ideal type or are composed of a mixture of elements from several genres. Neat lists of psalms that simply classify them according to genre ignore this reality.
- Form-critical descriptions necessarily concentrate on what is typical in a psalm, but the psalms also are compositions that incorporate distinctive literary elements important to their meaning. Focus on the typical may depreciate or ignore the individuality of a psalm.
- The reality of the Psalms as a book and the possibility that the location of a psalm in this literary context allows for an important interpretive perspective are not items on the agenda of approaches that only deal with the psalms singly and in groups created by genre.
- Comparison of Israel's psalms with apparent counterparts from other religions may lead to the conclusion that similarities in form and language may involve similarities in meaning and purpose. An interpretation that too easily equates the two misses the defining context of different cultural contexts and religions.

Gunkel was aware of these problems and referred to them in his magisterial work. Concern with them and their implications is currently shaping much that is developing in the study of the psalms. Approaches and perspectives that transcend and supplement form-critical and comparative methods are being tested. No one "method" is gaining dominance. Instead different experiments are being tried out in the attempt to cope with these problems.

CHANGES IN DIRECTION

Past research on psalms has characteristically focused on psalms grouped according to categories and on the setting for which psalms were originally composed. The leading questions have been: What are the genres of psalmic literature? To which genre should a particular psalm be assigned? What purpose did it serve in Israel's religion? In current scholarly work, attention is shifting to concern with individual psalms; to psalms as products of a process of preservation, reuse, and collection; and to psalms as part of a book. The earlier questions are not discounted, but there is a growing recognition that the psalms as we have them have been influenced by contexts other than the setting-in-life of their apparent genres and have undergone changes of meaning, purpose, and sometimes content. There is also significant interest in the book of Psalms as the final and sole directly available context of the psalms. Samples of what is afoot illustrate the features of the psalms receiving emphasis and furnish examples of what is being made of them.

A Psalm as an Individual Literary Composition

Though psalm criticism has tended to focus on the typical and to group psalms on the basis of their shared features, there is a renewed interest in the literary features that constitute a psalm's distinctive individuality. The conventions of a genre are not the only factor in the shaping of a psalm. Various modes of literary analysis allow the reader to discern and describe the poetic, stylistic, and rhetorical character of particular psalms.

Although Psalm 3 can be analyzed in terms of the typical elements of the individual lament, it constitutes a distinctive composition. It is composed of invocation and complaint (vv. 1–2), affirmation of confidence (vv. 2–6), petition (v. 7), a concluding sentence of praise of YHWH (v. 8a), and a blessing on YHWH's people (v. 8b). Nonetheless, this typical structure involves a distinctive literary workup. The threefold repetition of "many" unites and enforces the complaint. The affirmation of confidence balances statements about the psalmist's enactment of trust in the face of the "many." The psalm as a whole turns on the repeated theme of help (v. 2), deliver (v. 7), and deliverance (v. 8—all the same word in Hebrew); the psalm moves from a denial that God will save through an appeal for YHWH to save to a declaration that salvation belongs to YHWH. The literary shaping of the typical elements creates the individuality and theological substance of this psalm.

A Psalm as a Product of Israel's Religious Tradition

Although psalm criticism has been concerned primarily with the form in which and the use for which a psalm was first composed, more attention is now being given to the contribution of the transmission and continuing use of psalms to their identity and meaning. Features of the psalms not accounted for by generic criteria provide clues to a richer complex identity of the psalms. In the process of their transmission, psalms were used in settings different from the one for which they were composed. Psalms written for individuals were put to corporate use, and the elements of individual experience cited in prayers and thanksgivings became metaphors for corporate life. Some psalms were revised to adopt them for their use in different circumstances. Many were connected with David as a way to give psalms a context in Israel's emerging Scriptures. Psalms began to be composed out of the resources of the extant Scriptures. Psalm study has, of course, always been aware of this history, but its effect on the psalms is currently receiving much more attention.

Examples of such attention include the following: Psalm 30 belongs to the genre of "the thanksgiving song of an individual" who prayed for help and was delivered from death. Its superscription identifies the psalm as "a song of the dedication of the temple." This reclassification indicates that the psalm has been reread as a thanksgiving of Israel, since its corporate salvation is most likely with reference to the exile. In its present form the psalm has two identities and may be interpreted in two related but different contexts.

Psalm 102 seems to be a case of the rereading of a psalm by the literary process of expansion and intercalation. Its superscription identifies it as the prayer of an afflicted person. The psalm begins appropriately as the lament of an individual (vv. 1–11) and resumes the genre toward its end (vv. 23–24). But in its middle (vv. 12–22) and conclusion (vv. 25–28), the psalm turns to the corporate concern of Zion's restoration. The community is personified as the afflicted one. Either an individual lament has been revised by expansion for use as a community lament, or the genre of the individual lament has been used as a literary convention in the composition of a song for the congregation.

The superscription of Psalm 3 identifies this lament of one individual as "a psalm of David, when he fled from Absalom his son." Accordingly, the context in which the psalm is to be read is a portion of Scripture, the story in 2 Samuel 15. The superscription provides evidence of the process by which psalms were related to Scripture and by which they became Scripture. There was a late stage in the course of psalm composition when psalms were apparently composed drawing on extant Scripture. For instance, Psalm 103 reflects the influence of YHWH's self-proclamation in Exodus 34 on its composer (cf. Ps. 103:8

with Exod. 34:6–7). Psalm 119, the great poem on the law of the Lord, contains echoes of Deuteronomy, Jeremiah, Isaiah, and Proverbs. In extolling the instruction of the Lord, it uses Scripture as instruction.

A Psalm as Part of a Book

Although psalm criticism has interpreted psalms in the contexts of their genre and cultic setting, attention is also now being directed to the literary context of a psalm, that is, its location in the book of Psalms. Some question the assumption that the order and arrangement of psalms in the book is random or accidental. The relation of particular psalms to their immediate literary context and the possible coherence of sequences of psalms are being explored to see if there is a purposive or intentional ordering of the psalms. Some readers have discerned clues of vocabulary and theme that enable reading a psalm as part of a larger, meaningful context.

Psalm 8 can exemplify the significance of a psalm's particular literary location. It is the first hymn of praise in the book, set in a sequence of prayer psalms attributed to David. Psalm 7 ends with David's resolution to "sing praise to the name of the LORD, the Most High" (v. 17). Psalm 9 begins with a repetition of the resolution (vv. 1–2). Psalm 8 opens and closes with the praise of the name of the Lord, majestic in all the earth. In effect, "David" does in Psalm 8 what he promises in Psalms 7 and 9; the two frame Psalm 8 and explain what is happening in it. In turn Psalm 8 is a meditation on the importance of the human species to God and offers one theological explanation of why the prayers in the midst of which it stands are heard by God.

Psalms 113–118 offer an example of a sequence of psalms that can be read in a mutually interpretive way. As a group these psalms have a liturgical identity; they compose the Egyptian Hallel that was used in all the joyous festivals of Judaism and played a special role in the liturgy at Passover. The sequence is composed primarily of hymns of praise for the community, but 116 and 118 feature an unidentified individual. When the group is read in order, the unidentified "I" takes on the identity of personified corporate Israel. Several themes establish continuity and create an interpretive context in this sequence. Psalm 113 praises the Lord whose majesty is combined with mercy in raising up the lowly. Psalm 114 celebrates the Exodus as a manifestation of majesty acting in mercy, whereby the topic of the sequence is set as the Lord's way with Israel. Psalm 115 identifies the congregation who sings the psalms as Israel, house of Aaron and fearers of the Lord, and the nations as the problem that threatens them. In the face of the threat, Israel is to trust the Lord. The dead, says Psalm 115, do not praise the Lord, but Israel does. In Psalm 116 a singer gives thanks that the Lord in his mercy has saved him from death, and he promises to offer a sacrifice of thanksgiving and to call on the name of the Lord. Psalm 117 calls on the nations to praise the Lord because of the Lord's steadfast love shown to Israel. In Psalm 118 the promise is kept. The congregation composed of Israel, house of Aaron and fearers of the Lord, and personified as an individual who has been saved from death and who testifies that it is better to trust the Lord than human powers and nations, comes in the name of the Lord to give thanks to the Lord. By their position in the sequence, Psalms 116 and 118 are made into psalms of the community. Moreover, the theme of rescue from death that belongs to the songs of an individual is read as a metaphor for the salvation of the people of the Lord.

The Book of Psalms as a Book of Scripture

Historical criticism and form criticism paid little attention to the shaping and final shape of the book of Psalms. The opinion was held that the collection and arrangement of the psalms offer little for understanding individual psalms. That judgment was based on viewing the psalms as instances of a type and as agenda for cultic contexts. Those who also view the psalms as Scripture argue that what the psalms became and how they were understood in the process of making a book of Scripture have to be considered. The interest in the book as a whole and the shaping that created it is, of course, the larger dimension of the interest in the literary location of particular psalms. But it is by gaining a perspective on the whole that the various hermeneutical purposes that belong to the Psalms as a book of Scripture can be brought to light.

As various features of the macrostructure of the book are explored, it is becoming apparent that no one scheme comprehends the whole. The book seems to have been created by combining a succession of earlier stages. The approaches of redaction criticism, tradition-history, and canonical analysis are being used to see what can be discerned about these arrangements, the stages they represent, and their significance for the whole. Some important items on the agenda of investigation are the following: the introduction of the book by a psalm whose theme is the torah (law, instruction) of the Lord, and the division of the whole into five parts marked by doxologies. The appearance of a torah theme and vocabulary in a considerable number of psalms suggest an interest in shaping the book in analogy to the Torah of Moses to serve as complementary Scripture. The strategic location of psalms that deal with the anointed king points to a concern for the prophetic potential in texts about the messiah. The incorporation of two collections of the prayers of David, perhaps the earliest form of a Psalter, witnesses to the role the piety of the lowly played in creating the Psalter as an anthology of authorized prayers for all fearers of the Lord. Study of these and similar items may well converge in a comprehensive picture of the formation of the Psalter and the function of its final form as a hermeneutical context.

THE PROSPECT

In the coming decades, the study of psalms will likely follow the trends of the present. Form-critical and cult-functional approaches will continue to be established participants. But the interest in the literary distinctiveness of individual psalms, the transmission and composition of psalms through a history of successive traditions, and the formation and final form of the Psalter will enrich and broaden the perspectives in which psalms are interpreted. No single approach is likely to gain dominance. What psalm study has learned thus far is that the answer to the question "What is a psalm?" is complex. Any approach based on a single, simple answer will not be adequate to discern the rich and multivalent nature of a psalm.

Selected Bibliography

Introductions to Current Study of the Psalms
Day, John. *Psalms*. Old Testment Guides. Sheffield: JSOT, 1990.
Seybold, Klaus. *Introducing the Psalms*. Edinburgh: T & T Clark, 1990.

The Form-Critical Approach
Gunkel, Hermann. *The Psalms: A Form-Critical Introduction*. Biblical Series 19. Philadelphia: Fortress, 1967.
Westermann, Claus. *Praise and Lament in the Psalms*. Atlanta: John Knox, 1981.

The Cult-Functional Approach
Mowinckel, Sigmund. *The Psalms in Israel's Worship*. 2 vols. Oxford: Basil Blackwell, 1962.

The Psalms in the Context of the Ancient Near East
Keel, Othmar. *The Symbolism of the Biblical World: Ancient Near Eastern Iconography and the Book of the Psalms*. New York: Crossroad, 1985.

Literary Analyses of Psalms
Allen, Leslie C. *Psalms 101–150*. WBC 21. Waco, TX: Word Books, 1983.

Transmission and Scripturization
Mays, James L. "Going by the Book." In *The Lord Reigns*. Louisville, KY: Westminster John Knox, 1994.
McCann, J. Clinton, ed. *The Shape and Shaping of the Psalter*. JSOTSup 159. Sheffield: JSOT, 1993.
Wilson, Gerald Henry. *The Editing of the Hebrew Psalter*. SBLDS 76. Chico, CA: Scholars Press, 1985.

3

"Maker of Heaven and Earth"

Creation in the Psalms

In order to investigate the various ways creation is featured in the Psalter, it is necessary to identify at the outset the following eight items of consideration.

1. "Creation" in the sense frequently used today is not a notion that appears in the psalms. The term has come to mean no more than the natural world in the vocabulary of New Age religion, nature romanticism, environmental enthusiasm, artistic aestheticism, and even in unself-conscious traditional religion and liberal piety. There is no term or text in the psalms, indeed in the entire Bible, for creation in this sense.

2. The term "creation" can refer to an activity and to the outcome of the activity. It means, roughly, creating and what has been created. In the psalmic world of thought both verbal and nominal senses are always and specifically theological. The actor who creates is always YHWH, the God of Israel. What there is in creation is the Lord's making.

3. The topic of "creation," of making and of what has been made, is never an independent topic in the psalms; that is, it is never itself the subject of an entire psalm. It is rather a subtheme that is combined with other themes in the composition of psalms. There is nothing like what is found in Genesis 1–2, which is unique in this respect in the Bible. Psalm 104 comes closest, but its interest is more in providence than in creation.

4. The vocabulary of creation is quite simple and is largely shared with Old Testament literature in general. The following examples of words and phrases are illustrative:

Verbs

establish (*kwn*)   Pss. 8:3; 24:1; 93:1
make (*ʿśh*)   Pss. 33:6; 95:5

41

found (*ysd*)	Pss. 24:1; 89:11
form (*yṣr*)	Ps. 95:5
create (*brʾ*)	Ps. 104:30, the only instance

Nouns

earth/world (*ʾereṣ/tēbēl*)	Pss. 19:4; 24:1
heavens/earth (*šāmayim/ʾereṣ*)	Pss. 8:1; 57:5, 11
work(s) (*maʿăśeh*)	Ps. 104:24
creatures (*qinyān*)	Ps. 104:24

5. The famous phrase "YHWH, maker of heaven and earth" belongs to the provenance of psalmic literature (Pss. 115:15; 121:2; 124:8; 134:3; 146:5, 6). Outside the Psalter, it appears in the liturgical sentences in Genesis 14:5, 6. The phrase is confessional in function. The contexts in which the phrase appears show that its purpose is to identify YHWH as the deity who can help and bless the people of the Lord because of YHWH's power as creator of all that is. The creator's identity is firmly connected with the work of saving and blessing the congregation.

6. In the Psalms the making activity of YHWH is spoken of as an exercise of sovereignty. This active dominion is portrayed by several metaphors and poetic images, such as those of cosmic artisan (e.g., YHWH's hands formed the dry land [Ps. 95:5]) and cosmic monarch (e.g., YHWH spoke and it came to be [Ps. 33:6]). The most important portrayal, the one that furnishes a semantic and imaginative source for others, is the conflict scenario in which YHWH is victor over opposition (often the chaotic waters) and establishes the world as manifestation of divine rule; for example, YHWH rules the raging of the sea, scatters enemies, and founds heaven and earth as revelation of divine dominion (Pss. 89:5–18; 104:1–9).

7. It is important to note that the scenario and vocabulary used to speak of YHWH's making of heaven and earth are also employed in a collateral way to speak of YHWH's exercise of sovereignty in the affairs of nations and human beings. Note the use of the conflict scenario in Psalms 68, 74, and 77. Some texts place the cosmic and historical spheres in synonymously parallel positions (Pss. 65:7; 96:10). The vocabulary of making is used to describe the creation of both the world and the people of God (Ps. 95:5–7). Some psalms represent the activity of making the world and making the history of the people of God as linear (Pss. 136; 146; 147). The sovereignty that made the world is at work in the judging and saving of the world.

These seven considerations summarize the primary features of the way "creation" is conceived and spoken about in the psalms. But it is not through such ordered reviews that the topic engages the thinking, feeling, imagination, and reflection of those who read and sing the psalms as Scripture and liturgy. Rather, the topic is met in individual psalms where it is combined with other topics in a larger whole that furnishes a specific literary context. These specific contexts integrate the topic in a composition that has its own plan and purpose. The perspective shifts from psalm to psalm, each adding to the range and depth of the ways in which faith is instructed to view what is.

It is helpful, then, to look at specific psalms in order to inquire after their perspective. The general topic of "creation" is so comprehensive and complex that it seems best to sharpen selectively the subject and focus on "world" or "earth." The topic will be identified not just by the occurrence of the word pair "world/earth" but also by significant reference in the text to "world" and its constituents. The psalms explored in the following discussion are illustrative and certainly do not exhaust the possibilities. They provide examples of the ways in which "world" can be rendered in individual psalms. Particular attention will be given to literary features crafted into the composition, which will serve as guides to understanding the perspective on "world" that informs the psalm being read.

PSALM 8

Psalm 8 is the first in the Psalter in which world is a significant theme. Here "world" is envisioned as the manifestation of YHWH's majesty.

The subject of the psalm is stated in the choral line that opens and closes it as a defining inclusion: "O LORD, our sovereign, how majestic is your name in all the earth!" The sovereign to whom the worshipers sing this hymn has a royal identity throughout the earth! The vocabulary of royalty permeates the entire text: sovereign, majestic, glory, founded a bulwark (established power), crowned, glory and honor, and dominion. The psalm sees the whole earth bearing the signature of YHWH. Its vision is like that of the seraphic song "the whole earth is full of his glory" (Isa. 6:3). To be in the world is to be confronted with the reign and the ruling of the Lord.

The repetition of the second-person pronoun in the body of the hymn ("your," "you") ties everything mentioned to YHWH's name and majesty. In its exuberance the psalm views all in the heavens and on earth as radiant with the royalty of its creator. The psalm speaks of the world in direct address to YHWH. Hence, the world is incorporated in the I/thou idiom of praise.

The surprise in the psalm lies in the contrast between verses 1b–4 and 5–8. In the first section the majesty of YHWH would seem to belong to the realm above the earth. The splendor of YHWH is visible in the heavens. The sight of the night sky with its moon and stars overwhelms the psalmist in his human finitude. But the second section goes on to say that this humble human has been crowned with glory and honor, constituted with a royal domain. Notice the pairing of "work of your fingers" and "works of your hands" to refer respectively to the solar sphere and to the animal realm. Over the latter the human rules in analogy with YHWH's cosmic rule as a vassal establishment. There is a special perspective on "world" here. The world is the place where the human species knows its insignificance in the cosmos and is given its significance on earth. "The heavens are the LORD's heavens, but the earth he has given to [human beings]," says Psalm 115:16. The human being is given dominion by the divine realm, and that means accountability for as well as power over. The vision is admittedly anthropocentric and hierarchical. But not only is such a vision theologically inescapable, it is closer to reality and more pregnant with promise. In any case, according to the psalm's view it is in this human royal rule that the majesty of YHWH is present in all the earth. The hierarchies of the earth are a clue to the meaning of "world."

PSALM 24

Psalm 24 views the "world" as a place of accountability and expectation. It begins with a simple memorable couplet that states the essential and central declaration of the psalmic view of the world: "The earth is the LORD's and all that is in it, the world and those who live in it; for he has founded it on the seas, and established it on the rivers."

What makes Psalm 24 remarkable in its treatment of the world is what follows the introductory declaration of verses 1–2. Two more sections complete the psalm (vv. 3–6, 7–10). All three sections are so different in topic and style as to seem incoherent, yet their literary continuity with the opening declaration makes them serve as exposition to verses 1–2. In the context of the composition they assume the opening theme, which gives their content special significance.

The second section (vv. 3–6) reveals that the Lord, to whom the world and its inhabitants belong, has a special place in the world before which its inhabitants are accountable for their character and conduct. The world is not undifferentiated space. It is particularized by the Lord's relation to it, and the Lord's relation to persons is individualized by the particularizing of space into place. The world in the mode of "mountain of the LORD/holy place" translates the declaration about the Lord's sovereign universal relation to all into a question about the living of each person. The world, because it is the Lord's, is searchingly particular as well as inclusively universal.

The third section (vv. 7–10) declares that the world is where its sovereign wants to come and is coming. This owner of the world not only is above and beyond the world but wants to be in the world. It is the Lord's purpose to come as the "king of glory" who has won the battle over seas and rivers to found the world. Until the victor appears, it is not evident what the meaning of "world" is. Cosmic gates and sacred doors must open so that the sovereign who owns the world may enter and be present in the world. The liturgy of advent in verses 7–10 intones the meaning and destiny of the world. The world is where the kingdom of God is coming. "Lo, he stands at the door and knocks" (cf. Rev. 3:20).

PSALM 29

Psalm 29 envisions "world" as the theater of the glory of God. Although the word pair "earth/world" does not appear in the psalm, there is a compelling description of something happening in the world that bespeaks the truth about the world.

This psalm is in many ways a counterpart of and companion to Psalm 24. YHWH is called "king of glory," and a liturgy of entrance celebrates the king's coming as the victor who is strong and mighty in battle. In Psalm 29 YHWH is called "God of glory." The psalm describes an epiphany that is prophetic of YHWH's coming in the world. The unmistakable theme is "glory," established by its repetition in verses 1, 2, 3, and 9.

Glory is the visible appearance of power (vv. 1, 4). The compositional strategy of the psalmist is to employ a poetic description of a thunderstorm to portray power and evoke the experience of power (vv. 3–4). In the cultural world of the psalms the thunderstorm was virtually a classic medium for describing the divine victor whose victory over the counterforces of chaos brings about the world and manifests the reign of the deity. As often is the case in the tradition, the adversary is the primeval ocean, the mighty waters (vv. 3, 10). Here the poet has used the bending, flashing, shaking, reverberating, stripping effect of a thunderstorm's onset to evoke the direct experience of power, a power that surpasses the natural elements. This display of power is celebrated as a theologumenon of "the voice of the LORD," a motif repeated seven times, unifying the sequence of lines in verses 3–9. The imagery of the thunderstorm is used to visualize a power in the world that symbolizes the power that sustains the world.

Two significant notions concerning the world are presented by the use of the thunderstorm to represent the "voice of the LORD." Indeed, both are spoken in the concluding verses. Verse 10 proclaims, "The Lord is enthroned over the flood . . . as king forever." This poetic metaphorical declaration means that the powers of the physical world that coalesce and cohere to render the world extant and continuous are ordered by one supreme transcendent power. To behold the powers operative in the world is to behold refractions of the power that constitutes the universe. And the psalm knows its name (v. 2)! Verse 11 claims that this cosmic "king" whose name is the Lord is the source of strength and peace for his people. The people of the Lord have a cosmic connection. The very power that informs the universe with existence offers the people of God the coherence and constancy of *shalom*. The very strength that flows through the universe can flow through them to maintain order and future in the face of the floods of human history.

PSALM 65

Psalm 65 portrays the world as the farm of God. It evokes a fertility so abundant that the very earth and its produce transform themselves into a music of joy.

This theo-agricultural vision of earth does not appear in the psalm until verse 9. It occupies the final stanza of the hymn (vv. 9–13). It is preceded by two stanzas, each with its own topic. The first stanza comprises verses 1–4 and addresses God as God of the temple in Zion. The second consists of verses 5–8 and addresses God as the God of the cosmos. These first two stanzas each open with a vocative of identification, "God, in Zion" in the first and "God of our salvation" in the second. The third stanza contains no vocative at its beginning; it simply speaks to God directly. In the composition as a whole the identifications of the first two stanzas serve to say who the God is that is addressed in the third. In Israel it was theologically crucial that the God of the sanctuary and cosmos be the same as the God of fertility. Of course, the first two divine identities themselves have an inner connection with "world" in psalmic thought and form an important context for thinking about the world as the medium of divine goodness through fertility.

In the first stanza God engages the world through a place where divine presence is available. The focus is on Zion, courts, house, and temple. God is one to whom mortals may come. The availability is inclusive and universal: "all flesh" may approach. God's presence in his place means that God is there to answer prayer and forgive transgressions. There is goodness in this ministry to human finitude and fallibility that is the prime and first satisfaction of mortal neediness. By putting this stanza first, the psalm argues that the first joy in God is the nearness of the presence available in a special place in the world.

In the second stanza God is praised as the one whose strength is manifest in the existence of the world and what happens in the world. The two domains that God rules as sovereign are both in view here and interwoven in the composition of the stanza. The double dimension of God's relation to the world is specifically evident in verse 7: "You silence the roaring of the seas *and* the tumult of the peoples." The delivering events of salvation history and the cosmic signs of the world's stability and continuity are both reasons for hope and joy from one end of the earth to the other. This stanza places the joy in the knowledge of God as creator and savior alongside the joy in the presence of God in preparation for the final stanza.

Because of what has been said in the first two stanzas, God can be simply and directly addressed in the third as "you" ("thou"). In the opening thematic verse, the watering and enriching of the earth, by which grain is provided for its people, is acknowledged as the visitation of God. The rest of the stanza tells how God's visitation is at work from spring rains until abundant harvest takes on the appearance of joyous praise. The world is envisioned as the medium of God's satisfying goodness and personified as participant in God's praise.

Psalm 65 is a hymn of thanksgiving and has been used in liturgical tradition for harvest festivals and in services of thanksgiving. As such it puts the world in a significant perspective. The poetic vision of the psalm centers attention on God rather than on any assumed natural good fortune of the congregation, and insists on keeping every thanksgiving a liturgical occasion. It puts God's saving response to our neediness and sin first on the agenda and keeps the worshiper from slipping into self-satisfaction and self-congratulation over current well-being. The psalm shows that thanksgiving must take place in a universal setting; its reasons and possibilities belong even to those who live at earth's farthest bounds, thus correcting any proclivity to confine thanksgiving to the limits of a national identity. Finally, the psalm provides, especially for urban people, language to celebrate the goodness of the fertile earth and to view its provisions less in commercial and technical ways and more in relation to water, fields, and animals, the realia of world.

PSALM 98

Psalm 98 casts the world in the role of orchestra and choir to celebrate the coming of the Lord. In prophetic praise this hymn anticipates a time when the whole earth will resound with joy at the presence and rule of its rightful king.

The psalm is composed along the lines of the traditional formula for the imperative hymn: summons to praise and content or reason for praise. It begins with a brief summons (v. 1a) followed by the basis of the summons (vv. 1b–3); then calls to praise resume (vv. 4–8), to be concluded by a final statement of praise. The second and long series of imperatives that call to praise is divided into two stanzas by an inclusion ("Make a joyful noise to the LORD"), which marks off verses 4–6 as a separate stanza to create a hymn of three stanzas. A progressive line of thought runs through the whole. A new song must be sung to the Lord because God has done marvelous things; the marvelous things are the victory seen by the whole earth. The whole earth, therefore, should orchestrate praise before the Lord, whose right to be king has been vindicated in victory; even sea and earth are expected to join in the praise of the One who comes to rule the world with righteousness. The psalm is a hymn of praise to the One whose faithfulness to Israel is a revelation to the world of the sovereignty that is the destiny of the world.

When the synonyms "earth" and "world" are tracked through the lines of the hymn, certain perspectives on the world become apparent. Appearing in each of the three stanzas, one or both of the synonyms play a crucial role in the progression of thought. First, earth as the comprehensive place where the nations live is witness to the saving victory of the Lord; earth as the place where human history unfolds is the field on which the righteousness of Israel's God is revealed. Second, earth/world makes up the constituency of praise. Praise is no longer limited to Israel; it belongs to the world. Third, by the personified topography of the world, even the voiceless oceans and mountains are included in praise as a way of making the world's praise exhaustively inclusive. Fourth, the destiny of the earth is to be the realm of a righteous and equitable rule.

By its inclusion of the physical world of seas and hills in the performance of joyous praise, the psalm reflects a transformation in the way the earth's components are affected by the coming and action of the Lord. The pattern in the classic description of theophanies is a portrayal of the devastating impact of the appearance of God on the earth. Earth and its components melt, shake, are shattered, and so forth (e.g., 97:4–5). The shift from the reaction of awe and terror to the response of joyous acclamation shows that the coming of the kingship of the Lord into the world as savior transforms the very relation between God and created order. "For the whole creation awaits with eager longing for the revealing of the children of God" (Rom. 8:19).

PSALM 104

Psalm 104 is a hymn whose theme is the "works of the LORD." Its poetry offers us eyes to behold the world as wisdom.

More than any other psalm, Psalm 104 is occupied with the topic of creation in general and the world in particular. It is composed of two major sections, each beginning with a vocative address to the Lord and a summary statement of praise (v. 1b introducing vv. 2–23 and v. 24a introducing vv. 24–25). The first section opens with yet another portrayal of the Lord as cosmic monarch who has gained dominion in the heavens by the power manifest in the thunderstorm (vv. 1–4) and has established the earth by driving the waters off its surface and containing them in their appointed places (vv. 5–9). From these contained waters, the Lord makes springs and streams to flow so that "the earth is satisfied with the result of your works" (vv. 10–13). The first section concludes with an extended recitation of the features of life in the earth, which serves as an exposition of the satisfactoriness of the works of the Lord, who has provided food, habitat, and times for living things (vv. 14–23). The second section begins with an exclamation over the variety of the Lord's works and an illustration of that variety (vv. 24–26). Then the psalmist reflects on the dependence of all these creatures on the providence of the Lord (vv. 27–30) and concludes with a wish-prayer that the Lord may rejoice in creation as the psalmist rejoices in the Lord (vv. 31–35).

The psalm looks at the world as the work of the Lord's wisdom. "Wisdom" is the combination of knowledge, understanding, and capacity that makes one competent for the task at hand. "World," as the sum of the "works" of the Lord, is a display of such wisdom (v. 24). Note how the term "your works" is used at strategic points for the world and all that is in it (vv. 13, 24, 31). Note also that the description of the cosmic victor includes the motif of building (v. 3) and ordering things to their appointed place (vv. 8–9). In the poetic portrait of the world in verses 10–23, everything has its provender, its place, and its time. Everything coheres. All are interrelated in the great web of works of the Lord. To watch the wild animals, to enjoy a glass of wine, to see birds building their nests, or to observe the rhythm of the passing of day and night is to sense and wonder and revel at the wisdom of it all. This dimension of the psalm comes quite close to the environmental ecological sensibility of modern times that knows from observation and accumulated experience how exquisitely interrelated the world is. Only the secular mind misses the transcendent power informing it all.

The psalm discloses the continuity between creation and providence, between the making of creatures and provision for their existence. The earth that the Lord has set on its foundations is depicted as a vast habitat. The Lord's creative activity continues through the shaping of the cosmos and the bringing forth of the earth from the primeval waters into the watering, feeding, and situating that make it possible for creatures to live. It is not too much to say that life itself is, in the view of the psalm, the crowning purpose of creation. The total dependence of life on the works of the Lord, described by the psalm in its best-known section (vv. 27–30), points finally to the integration of every life form into the great process of making and supporting. Life and death, death and life, together witness that creation continues in the world.

In the way that it speaks of the human species (Heb. ʾādām, NRSV "people") the psalm puts us in our place, so to say. "Adam" is arranged along with cattle and other animals in dependence on the great process of providence;

humanity's activities are set in conformity to the calendars of the world (vv. 14–15, 20–23). The human species is simply one more of the creatures, with and among them, in contrast to its position at the apex of the created hierarchy in Psalm 8. All our similarities to the animals indicate how much we are a part of the world. The human position of authority and responsibility does not promote us above the ranks of creature. Knowing the world is knowing self, and knowing self is knowing the world. Our living and dying are knit together in the Lord's way with the world.

Verse 35 must not be overlooked. It says that in the world known as the works of the Lord wickedness is a shocking and unacceptable incongruence. Wickedness, whether in others or in self, is a jarring, discordant note in the praise that alone is an adequate response to the world as the work of the Lord. So the psalm will not end without raising the question for the reader about accountability for what distorts the great system of life from its purpose of reflecting on the wisdom of God and responding with prayer and conduct, "Bless the LORD, O my soul."

CONCLUSION

There are, of course, other psalms in which one may discover perspectives in which world is viewed. Psalm 19, with its opening declaration that the heavens are revealing the glory of their creator, is a well-known example. Like Psalm 24, Psalm 19 is composed of three quite different parts, which together point to the incompleteness of the revelation of God's glory in the heavens. While the glory is visible in the created world, the salvific word is heard only through the torah of the Lord, which calls humans to self-knowledge and reliance on the divine. The glory beheld by the eye supports the word heard by the ear and drives the heart to prayer. Psalm 148 uses the word pair "heavens/earth" as a compositional device: the first half of the psalm calls for everything in the heavens to praise the Lord; the second half calls for everything on the earth to praise the Lord. Praise in the world is united with praise above the world so that the name of the Lord is declared as the truth about all reality. In such ways the topic "world" is incorporated into psalmic poetry that the Spirit can use to open the eyes of our spirit to see what otherwise we could not. There is more to this world through whose places and times we blunder than ever our unaided imaginations would surmise. There are, however, good reasons to believe that the one to whom this paper is written to honor and thank is more likely than most to discern the world in psalmic vision.

4

The Self in the Psalms and the Image of God

The Bible is about God and the human being. From Genesis to Revelation the subject is God and humanity. In all its books and literary genres Scripture tells about God's way with human beings and their life in the world. It can be read as a vast theological anthropology. In its theocentricity it is anthropocentric. Any of the Bible's texts can serve as a source for reflection on the human identity and condition.

This essay is a reading of one set of interconnected texts, beginning with a cluster of texts that contain self-descriptions by endangered persons: the prayers for help in the book of Psalms. The prayers are chosen as a pivotal and organizing group of texts because the loss of what we call "human dignity" and hope of its restoration are essential features of their composition. Questions and clues emerging from the self-descriptions in the prayers lead to a hymn intercollated in them, Psalm 8. The hymn with its description of the glory and role of the human being in the creation calls for a consideration of the first chapters of Genesis as the prolegomenon necessary to reading the psalms. Finally, the connection between the psalmic prayers and the crucial metaphor of the image of God on the one hand and the portrayal of the identity and role of Jesus Christ on the other leads to texts in the Epistles and Gospels. The purpose of this essay is to put the subject of the worth of the human being and the hope of its realization in the perspective of this complex of texts.

THE PRAYERS OF THE BOOK OF PSALMS
The Prayers for Help as Witness to the Human Condition

In the Twenty-second Psalm there is an arresting disavowal. In the course of describing his affliction the psalmist says, "I am a worm and not a human being

[Heb. *ʾîš*]" (v. 8). This painful negation in its sharp brevity assumes a conviction about what it means to be a human being. The very experience of deprivation evokes a consciousness of what has been lost that is epitomized in the mournful cry, "not a human." The description of trouble that forms the context of this negation identifies what it is that diminishes his hold on his identity as "human," and as well what its recovery requires. "Human" in the psalmist's vocabulary is not a biological classification. It is instead an existential identity that is realized and enacted in living. It is an awareness of what one is that can be lost and can be restored.

This exclamation about one's identity as "human" and its loss is a witness to what is going on in the prayers for help that compose the stock of the book of Psalms. By far the majority of the psalms are, to use the genre customary in form criticism, laments of an individual.[1] They are prayers for help by a beleaguered and beset person. They record the voice of a person addressing God, describing the woes that afflict his existence, pleading for deliverance and anticipating restoration. There is also a smaller subset of prayers of thanksgiving by a person who has been delivered from trouble and a few prayers of trust in the face of danger. Along with the individual laments there is a much smaller group of similar corporate prayers. All of these genres share formal features, motifs, and purposes. The others are all internally related to the individual prayers for help as their center of gravity. Even the hymns in the Psalter have an inner relation to the prayers in a way that holds the whole together in a rhetorical and theological coherence.

The psalmic prayers for help are a virtually unique access to the self-understanding of a human being in the biblical world. Nowhere else in Scripture is the first-person voice heard in such frequency and continuity as here. In the course of pleading for help an "I" speaks to a "you" about "them" and "me" and "you." If the notion of "self" can be said to represent a consciousness that can employ personal pronouns, then these prayers are poignant disclosures of "self."[2] Though the prayers employ the vocabulary and categories and relationships of their culture and its traditions, they nonetheless reveal contours of a self that transcends a particular era. They are an eloquent testimony to a view of human beings, its conditions and necessities and potentials.

It is not only their character and content that make the prayers for help important texts for theological consideration of the human condition. The psalmic prayers have a double role in Jewish and Christian practice. They are Scripture and are used for instruction about God and God's way with the world and human beings. The prayers are also liturgy, prayers, and praise that are said and sung in worship and rehearsed in the exercises of contemplation. When used for liturgy and devotion the self in the psalmic prayer speaks through the mind and voice of believers.[3] The "I" of the prayer finds voice through the believer and in the process involves the user in the constitutive neediness and aspiration of the self in the prayers. Through their use the self whose voice is there in the psalm is always potentially a conditioning reality for the self-understanding of those who hear and say them. One has only to think of the role of the psalms in Augustine's confessions or Bonhoeffer's meditations to find witnesses to this interface of the psalmic and personal self. So the way in which the psalms disclose the human condition continues through their use as Scripture and liturgy to inform and guide believers to self-discovery and expression.

In turning to the psalmic prayers as a resource for thinking about and living the human identity it is important to read them for what they are. The psalms are largely cultic texts that were originally designed for specific liturgical usage. The prayers were composed for individuals, perhaps often a royal figure, to use at sanctuary sites. The composers were likely professionals, steeped and gifted in the oral and literary genres of worship. Little is known about the precise character of the ceremonies in which the prayers were used. So these prayers, of course, are not informed by an anthropology in any scientific sense. Their idiom is poetry and their language elusive and multivalent in reference. Their topic is the one who prays and praises. In their portrayals of need and hope for help the psalms do record in a language shaped by tradition what it is like to be a human being. Their utterance expresses assumptions and convictions that answer questions about the nature and identity of a self. A knowledge of "who and what I am" informs their speech.

It is also important, as will be attempted in this study, to think about the psalmic prayers in their literary and canonical context. What is said about the self who speaks in them both assumes and is to be interpreted by what is said in the other psalms that compose their semantic environment and by the connections that inhere in them with other parts of Scripture. The inscripturalization of the psalms in the formation of the book of Psalms and in the formation of the Jewish and Christian canon of Scripture provides the thought-world in which they have been and are to be read.

The Typology of the Self of the Prayers

The individual whose voice is heard in the first-person-singular psalms is not a particular person. The distinct specific experience of those for whom the prayers were composed is interpreted and described through the conventions of a mode of prayer that had been nurtured in Israel's long history with its God. Because the vocabulary employed to describe the experience of trouble is conventional and formulaic, it is difficult to determine just what trouble occasions a particular prayer. The language can imply illness or alienation from the community through false accusation or the threatening hostility of others or personal failure and guilty conscience or combinations of such troubles.

The self speaks through a combination of vocabulary and literary elements that belong to the genre of individual prayers for help.[4] The selection of language and the arrangement of literary elements vary from prayer to prayer; this creative variation of common features produces the particular prayers in their distinctness. But the function and language of the elements are so typical as to form a kind of template through which the self of those using the prayers is presented. The one who prays is given a self through which to be present to God.

Through all the variety in the prayers there is a sense in which the self who speaks is the same self. The presence of this paradigmatic self in all the prayers makes it possible to draw general observations about the representation of the self in all of them.

The typical elements of the individual prayer for help are as follows: The prayers usually begin with a vocative that names the one to whom the prayer is addressed. In a description of trouble the one praying speaks of self in terms of a neediness that is the reason for the prayer. The description typically refers to a neediness in relationship to God and self and others, and follows a pattern of the three personal pronouns, "you/I/they." A petition forms the central organizing element. The petition is usually twofold, a plea to be heard and to be helped. A motive stating reasons that the prayer should be heard is frequently attached to the petition. An affirmation of trust confesses confidence in God and God's help. Usually, the prayer concludes with praise of God, either expressed or promised or anticipated.

Psalm 13 has long been recognized as an almost formulaic illustration of these typical elements and their use.[5]

Elements	Psalm 13
Vocative	LORD
Description of trouble	
Second person–you–God	How long will you still forget me; How long hide your face from me?
First person–I–self	How long must I bear pain in my soul, And sorrow in my heart all day long?
Third person–they–others	How long shall my enemy be exalted over me?
Petition	
To be heard	Consider and answer, LORD, my God.
To be helped	Give light to my eyes,
Motive	Or I will sleep the sleep of death, And my enemy will say, "I have won."

Affirmation of trust	But I trust in your steadfast love; My heart will rejoice in your salvation.
Praise	I will sing to the LORD, Because he has done good for me.

Because these literary elements are so consistently used in the composition of the prayers and their related genres, they imply a set of attributes of the human self that is expressed in them. The profile of the self that is sketched by the prayers is, of course, conditioned by the use for which they were composed. They belong to situations in which the self is endangered or at least conscious of endangerment, but perhaps it is in times of such awareness that the contours of the self come into clearest expression. Because of this their articulation of an instance of human affliction is based on the actuality of the human and a view of its condition.

1. The prayers are the artifacts of a creature that can translate consciousness into communication. Of course any writing or speech or conversation is an example of the linguisticality of the human animal. But the prayers are particularly evident instances of the capacity to move what the self experiences beyond the experience itself, so that self-consciousness transcends the self. When language becomes the form that the experience of endangerment takes, something essential is disclosed about this creature. It can move physical and mental pain from the sensory and psychic sphere to the sphere of language. What is felt is brought into reach of will and thought, of memory and anticipation. Through the language the self knows that it is more than the naked experience of affliction. There is a self that can set it forth, establish even a little distance, view it, and speak about it.

2. The prayers exhibit the self as a relational reality. The consciousness of the self in them comes to expression with the use of the personal pronouns. The style is mostly direct address; an "I" speaks to a "you" about the you and I and a "they." The prayers disclose a self whose consciousness as an I is congruent with a consciousness of others. Even when the one who prays speaks specifically of himself, the speaking is said to another. The prayers support an understanding of the human self as constituted by its social relationships.

3. The prayers portray a self that exists in three spheres: physical, social, and theological. The threefold pattern of descriptions of trouble is based on the three spheres. The agenda of the descriptions is typically physical and mental affliction, the harmful effect of others, and the absence or wrath of God. The self is an embodied self that feels and thinks. It is a social self whose individual personhood is inextricably involved in a community of others. It is also a religious self that by individual intuition and given traditions needs and depends on a power transcendent of the human realm. In the way that the prayers speak in these three constitutive contexts of the self it is clear that they

are interdependent, each conditioning the others. God, others, and the body are the skeins of which the fabric of the praying consciousness is woven.

4. The prayers are the expression of an inherent neediness of the self. The petitions as the formal expression of the neediness are pleas to be heard and helped. A variety of imperatives are used, such as "heal me," "deliver me," "be gracious to me." The petitions seek relief from the troubles that are the occasions for the prayer: restoration of physical well-being, protection and vindication before hostile others, reintegration into the community, acceptance by God, and freedom and cause to rejoice in praise. All these various needs are indications that the relational self is a dependent self. With dependence comes vulnerability. From time to time the psalmist offers a simple description of the self: "I am poor and needy." The assertion does not refer to economic deprivation. It is rather a confession that existence is structured by finitude and fallibility. Even where physical and social dangers are relieved, the psalmist will say of himself, "I am poor and needy."

5. The prayers argue that the essential neediness of the human self is for the person and presence of God. The self of the psalms is inextricably religious in a way that includes and transcends the physical and social dimensions of its existence. The prayers are addressed to the divine You as the one who can maintain the self. They are the expression of a consciousness that includes in its nature an expectation of a transcendent being heard. The way in which needs of the physical, psychological, and social spheres are presented shows that they involve the religious need. The pain of the various empirical problems is ultimately their effect on the consciousness of God. The urgency of the resolutions requested is their power to renew the personal knowledge of the divine. In all the prayers, what the human "I" seeks is the divine "You." That God in and through and beyond all else is the need is always assumed and at times poignantly said in such confessions as, "Whom have I in heaven but you? / And there is nothing on earth that I desire other than you" (Ps. 73:25).

The Prayers as Witnesses to Human Identity and Worth

There are problems to be recognized in using the psalmic prayers as a resource in a contemporary discussion of anthropology. The prayers are the product of a specific historical culture that qualifies and limits the notions that their composers employed. In their present form they are attributed to a particular individual and related in some cases to episodes in his life. "Human" as adjective and noun in a taxonomic or moral sense is not part of their vocabulary. Nor is the worth of the individual self grounded in a natural or political status belonging to the individual as such.

In reading the prayers as documents of the self, however, it is important to remember that as a genre of human speech they are part of a larger general literature. The lament-prayer was not unique to Israel but was composed and used across the religious cultures of the time and region of which Israel's history was a part.[6] Many of the conventions and much of the vocabulary used to describe the troubles of the self in the psalms appear to have been part of this ecumenical genre. This broader setting for the genre and its typical features are evidence that the self-descriptions in the psalms participate in an "anthropology" that represents the experience of a wide and inclusive population. The self who speaks in the prayers is, of course, an Israelite self whose religious and moral consciousness is shaped by Israel's history with the God it came to know through that history. The psalmists pray as members of a selected people, and their prayers are informed by a particular knowledge and obligation that belongs to that special identity, but their prayers are a version of a general genre and a way of their liturgical participation in a larger humanity that is represented by the self described in the psalms.

Another factor in the paradigmatic character of the self in the prayers is the complexity of its identity.[7] Most of the prayers are introduced as the words of David, the prototypical messianic king whose story is told in the books of Samuel. It is evident from the redaction of the psalms and the formation of the book that the postexilic community used the prayers as expressions of its corporate identity. It is reasonably certain the prayers were as a type originally composed and used by particular hurting Israelites. After the final formation of the book the psalms composed in first person were read and used by individuals in the community. It is a continuation of this flexible construal that in the Christian tradition the self in the prayers has been understood as a Christian worshiper or as the corporate church or as Christ.

The prayers do reflect a clear, strong sense of self-worth that is wounded and weakened by the trouble described. The lament in Psalm 4:2 is almost thematic: "O men, how long shall my honor (*kabod*) suffer shame?" References to "shame/be ashamed" and "humiliate/be humiliated" as ways of speaking about injury to self-worth are scattered through the Psalms (Pss. 25:3; 31:2; 35:4; 37:19; 40:15–16; 44:16; 69:7, 8, 20, 21; 70:3, 4; 71:1, 13, 21, 25). "Honor/glory" (*kabod*) is used for the sense and status of worth that the self claims and cherishes in the few cases in which it is spoken of specifically (Pss. 4:2; 7:5; 16:9; 62:7; 84:11). In these instances it is made clear that the honor claimed by the praying self derives from, is dependent on, and can be restored by God. Shame is experienced by the self in its social setting, but honor is restored by the deliverance of God. The psalmist can even say, "But you, O LORD, are a shield around me, my glory, and the one who lifts up my head" (Ps. 3:3).

THE CANONICAL CONTEXT OF PRAYERS

Psalm 8 and the Prayers

How these Israelite psalmists came to claim that God and a relation to God is the reality of their sense of self-worth, the prayers do not explain. But there is a hymn, Psalm 8, which does.[8] Typical of the hymns in the Psalter, the Eighth Psalm has as its subject what God is like and does. It is woven into the collection of prayers that compose books 1 and 2 of the Psalter as if its place there were necessary. The theme stated at its beginning and end is the majesty of the name of the Lord. The theme echoes the close of Psalm 7 and the opening of Psalm 9–10 in a way that shows that they are combined into a larger literary unit. This larger whole has been edited into an interrelated context for reading.

Psalm 8 declares what the prayers assume. The glory and honor of mortals are the endowment of God. But what the hymn says about the endowment is not coherent with the identity of the self and the condition of humanity as described in the prayers.

The hymn praises God for the creation of humankind and speaks of the human being as the work of God. Humanity is described as God made it to be. The description of God's action in making the human species is composed with the use of a metaphor. God's creative act is portrayed as the inauguration of an official in a royal administration. The Lord appears as sovereign of the universe whose majesty pervades all the earth. The making of the human consists of appointment to a rank, bestowal of recognition, and assignment of a role. Humankind is installed at a level just below the *ᵓelohim*, the divine members of God's court and administration. The dignity and importance of the human being are marked by the bestowal of glory and honor, attributes of divine and human royalty. The assigned role is responsibility for one sector of God's creation, all other living creatures.

So the construing context for the significance and worth of humankind is "the kingdom of God." The human, corporately and individually, bears and wears the glory and honor of God in the created world. The species is portrayed as a vassal of the divine rule. What it is and does is a representation of God's reign. Its dominion is intended to correspond to the divine sovereignty and is ordained to conform to God's will and way. Thus, humankind derives its identity and destiny from its relation to God. The relationship is not formal and external. It is constitutive of what creature the human being is. Apart from that relation humankind has no ultimate meaning different from other creatures.

In his reflective praise the psalmist wonders, "What is man that you are mindful of him, / and the son of man that you care for him?" The psalmist's assertion that the human being is created for the kingdom of God in the world is the answer to the question. It is by and through the human being that the reign of God is honored and glorified in the world. The human species, corporately and individually, is the project of God's kingdom. That is the unstated authorizing foundation of the prayers for help. God's endowment and purpose are at issue where the glory and honor of human beings are ignored and obscured.

Psalm 8 speaks about the entire human species, about "man" as everyman. The individual of the prayers speaks very much as one of these human beings, but not just as anyone. The self of the prayers is a person whose sense of self is shaped by the memory of a particular people and its traditions. The "I" has a special personal relationship to God who is called "YHWH," the name of Israel's covenant deity, and is addressed as "my God" (e.g., Pss. 3:7; 5:2; 22:1–2). The supplicant identifies himself to God as "your servant" as a way of claiming a right to be heard (e.g., Pss. 27:9; 31:16; see also 34:22; 35:27).

Moreover, the picture of humanity reflected in the prayers is that of a fractured and flawed race. The corporate humanity crowned with glory and honor and ordained to dominion over other creatures is distorted. The destiny of corporate dominion is being realized in the domination of some human beings by others. In the prayers framing Psalm 8, hostility, affliction, and oppression mark the human scene. Human conduct features arrogance, ruthlessness, and cunning. The predominant human corporate identities are self-seeking autonomous nations. We read of those whose actions deny the reality of God (Ps. 10:3-4), of a terrorizing "man . . . of the earth" (Ps. 10:18), and of petitions that mortals not succeed in domination (Ps. 9:19).

The dissonance between the hymn's portrayal of created humankind and the hymn's contexting prayers' testimony to historical humankind is deafening. There is a tragic incongruence between what God has created and the human being has wrought. The royalty conferred on the human being by God has become the kingdoms of this world in which it is forgotten "that they are but men" (Ps. 9:20). Mortals turn the need for God into greed (Ps. 10:3) and the glory given by God into pride (Ps. 10:4). Reading the Eighth Psalm in the midst of the prayers evokes its eschatological tension. In its present place in the midst of the prayers it locates the human as it is created to be in the midst of humanity as it is. Historical humanity is between creation and realization, living an unfulfilled destiny in a flawed and perverted way.

The protological account of this dissonance is of course recorded in the sequence of chapters 1 and chapters 2–3 of Genesis. Psalm 8 is a poetic version of Genesis 1:26–28. The story of a humanity that leaves Eden (Gen. 2–4) to live the curse instead of the blessing, to murder the brother, and to fashion culture as a temple of self-assertion instead of as room for the Presence is the necessary canonical preface to the enigmatic humanity portrayed in the prayers.

The Image and Likeness of God

In Genesis 1:26–27 the nature and worth given to human beings by divine creation is designated by the term "image of God." The notion has always been the central theme of theological anthropology.[9] From the patristic to the modern period Christian theology has connected the dignity of human nature with the theme of the image of God. The inclination has been to define the concept in terms of capacities and attributes such as reason, will, knowledge, righteousness, happiness, and so on, that could be reasonably inferred from the term and other texts of Scripture. But there is broad agreement currently that the biblical text does not elaborate the term in such a way. Verses 26f. simply use the words "image" and "likeness" to designate a relation of the human being to God in the human's created nature. The designations apply to both genders of the species and assign dominion over the other creatures as the role of the so-created human being.

When the usage of these defining words is examined in other texts their meaning is clear enough, and it is a reasonable assumption that Genesis 1:26–27 would be read in a way consistent with these other uses.[10] "Image" (selem) is used for representations of a deity (Num. 33:52; 2 Kgs. 11:18//2 Chr. 23:17; Amos 5:26; Ezek. 7:20; 16:17); for a likeness of mice and tumors (1 Sam. 6:5–11) and for a likeness to man (Ezek. 23:14), all in reference to cultic settings; and once for shadows as fleeting reflections of people (Ps. 37:9). In its twenty-five occurrences "likeness" (demut) consistently means "similar to, but not the same as." In what the similarity consists depends on context (e.g., Ezek. 1:5; Dan. 10:16; 2 Kgs. 16:10; Isa. 40:18). In the repetition of Genesis 1:26 in Genesis 5:1–2 "likeness" replaces "image," and in 5:3 the order of the two terms is reversed so as to imply that the two are regarded by the writer as virtual synonyms. Here the terms are also used to describe the relation of Seth to his father, Adam. The meaning is not, however, that Seth looked like Adam, but that which in Adam made him an image/likeness of God is passed on in the generational process. It is specific to the species, not alone to the individual first man.

The last use of "image of God" as identification of the created nature of human beings occurs in the context of God's instruction of Noah after the flood (Gen. 9:6). The fact that human beings are made in the image of God is said to be the reason that the life of each person requires ultimate respect from others. The attribute, "image of God," belongs to an individual of the species as well as to the species as a whole. It is what gives each person worth. The postdiluvian setting of this text also shows that the image of God belongs to the human being beyond and through all the drastic failures of mortals recorded in Genesis 3–9.

When read in the light of Psalm 8, Genesis 1:26–28 appears to be based on the same rank and role pattern of identification featured in the hymn's use of a metaphor of royal ordination and installation. The rank in the psalm is "little less than *Elohim* [the divine beings?]" and in Genesis it is "image of *Elohim*." The role in both is dominion over the creatures. The plural style of the self-exhortation "let us" and of "our image" almost certainly indicates that the notion of the divine royal court staffed by the *Elohim* in which God exercises his sovereignty in relation with the human world is assumed by the text.[11] The specification of male and female and the use of the plural "them" to refer to "man" is a way of including both genders in the image-identity rather than an indication of what the image-identity is. The identification of the human being as the image of God belongs to the deep and rich tradition of thinking about God's relation to the universe as a divine sovereignty that is thematic for the breadth of Scripture. The human rank and role in the world corresponds to that of God over the world. Psalm 115:16 remarks that "the heavens are the LORD's heavens, but the earth he has given to [humankind]," yet another specification of spheres of authority and responsibility as constitutive of the human.

What the "image of God" texts in Genesis and those related to them claim is that the relation of representation and resemblance to God is constitutive of human created nature. It is not separable but part of human nature. It holds for the species and individuals in it. It is central and foundational to the biblical view of God's way with the world as anthropocentric.

The Other Likeness

The texts concerning humanity as image of God all appear in Genesis 1–11, a narrative complex that has the protological formation of humankind as its subject. The complex contains a second account of creation in chapters 2–3, which with chapter 1 form a double introduction to the complex. This second account features another likeness of human beings to the Elohim (Gen. 3:5, 22). This likeness is not a representing and resembling God in the matter of God's sovereignty, but rather the opposite. It stands in tension with the created likeness. This likeness consists of "knowing good and evil."

In the story told in Genesis 2–3 the knowledge of good and evil is the fruit of the forbidden tree that stands in the center of the garden (Gen. 2:9, 17), so it is a divinely prohibited possibility for human beings. It is a consummation promised and realized by the contradiction of God (Gen. 3:1, 4). It is the autonomous prerogative to decide what is nourishing and beautiful and best for living life (Gen. 3:6). The acquisition of this knowing evokes a self that is self-conscious before others and afraid of God (Gen. 3:7, 10). It results in an experience of life where blessing is distorted by curse (Gen. 3:14–19).

"Like Elohim, knowing good and evil," means assuming divine autonomy in discerning and deciding what is beneficial to life and what is detrimental.[12] The expression does not refer to the capacity of reason and its use, but to a misuse of reason that is centered radically in the self. When the Lord God says, using the plural style of self-reference again, "Behold, the human being has become like one of us, knowing good and evil," the sovereignty of God and its mythic setting in the divine court is again alluded to (Gen. 3:22; see 1:26). God is sovereign over life and living. The issue of human life and death is thematic in the story of Eden. God is source, support, and limit of human life (Gen. 2:7, 9; 3:4, 14, 17, 22). That the human being should claim independent sovereignty over life puts the human in conflict with the divine (Gen. 3:22).

After its twofold introduction the narrative complex of Genesis 1–11 unfolds its account of the formation of humankind. The human as protagonist of history is portrayed in stories and genealogies. The themes are relationships and alienations: between genders, siblings, occupations, parents and children, kindred, languages, nations, and throughout the narrative sequence between the human being and God. The stories are all a sequel to Genesis 3:22. They concern a corporate and individual self that has become its own center and reference in the matter of life and death. Twice in the narrative sequence there are reminders that this self is a God-imaged creature (Gen. 5:1–2; 9:6), but nothing in the telling reconciles the contradiction between the two likenesses of God and humanity. The creation of the human being to represent and resemble God's sovereignty in the world seems to be a given of human identity, but a given of an essential destiny that has to be realized. The self-centered enterprise to take possession of life is a radical disconnection with the original likeness. The two identify the human creature in their contradiction, and the contrast between the two is the analog and theological preface to the disparity between the prayers for help and their explanatory hymn. If one begins with Genesis 1–11 to learn about the human condition, the disparity between Psalm 8 and its companion prayers for help is no surprise.

Representation and Likeness as Call and Promise

It is an apparent anomaly that "image of God" does not recur in the rest of the Old Testament. As crucial as it is in the account of the Beginnings, the phrase as identification of the human being disappears, leaving its one poetic echo in Psalm 8. In Genesis 12:1–3 a further identification of human beings beyond creation is inaugurated by God. It is a particular identity constituted by a command and a promise. The command is a call to a future that God will provide; the promise is a history of greatness in which God offers to all humankind the lost blessing purposed at creation. From Genesis 12 forward the biblical story focuses on particular identities of human beings created by command and promise. These further identities become the surrogate enactors of the value and significance of human beings. Corporately and individually these further identities are people of God, covenant people, servants of God. In the biblical story the rest of humanity, social groups and nations and individuals, are viewed in relation to these identities created by the command and promise of God.

While "image of God" is no longer used for the human being in the biblical story, its actuality is a structural theme of the biblical account of God and humankind. The actuality continues in the calling and destiny of human beings to represent and resemble God in the world. When this calling and destiny is given to some, it assumes and continues the purpose and possibility vested in the creation of humankind. The pivotal defining text is Exodus 19:3–6, God's inaugural words to Israel as a covenant people. Israel is given a role and destiny to represent and resemble God among the peoples of the world. Through an existence defined by the demands and promise of the covenant, Israel will have a particular and special relation to the Lord as God's priestly kingdom and holy nation who represent God's sovereignty over all the earth. The corporate people are even referred to as "son" of God (Exod. 4:22; Hos. 11:1). Their corporate and individual life is to resemble the God whose they are. The primary divine attributes of holiness, righteousness, justice, and loving-kindness are the ethical responsibility of the people, a responsibility urged by exhortations like "You shall be holy, for I the LORD your God am holy" (Lev. 19:2). Within the people of God the Davidic messianic king especially is given the role of representing and resembling God, first of all to his subjects but also to the nations. He is called "Son of God." He is to exemplify the attributes and do the work of the Lord. Dominion is his vocation; righteousness, justice, and peace are his tasks. All humankind in their historical identity as "the nations" are his domain (see Pss. 2; 18; 20; 21; 72; etc.).[13]

The story of Israel as told in the Old Testament is broadly a sequel to Genesis 1–11. Israel is a part of the humanity described there, and its career concerns all humankind. The identity and destiny of the people of the Lord is a movement toward the realization of humanity's identity and destiny as image of God.

THE PRAYERS IN CONTEXT

The psalmic prayers need to be read in light of this deep background and in the context of the biblical story. They are the prayers of a creature created to be the image and likeness of God, a self that seeks life by knowing good and evil, an individual in community chosen and called to be the servant of God.

As creatures whose destiny and identity is to represent and resemble God in the matter of God's sovereignty, the psalmists bear an indissoluble relation to God. The prayers are the expression of an intimation of dependence that informs all human beings, whether denied or confessed, a longing that cannot be satisfied within and by the self alone. The prayers arise out of an inherent need for meaningfulness for existence, a compulsion of the self to find its own meaning in mastery of the world and its creatures. The psalmists pray out of an ineradicable instinct of human significance in the world. In them a self pleads for the attention that is due the one to whom the central place within creation belongs.

As the "living beings" of Genesis 2:7 the psalmists want to live. The prayers come from a self whose deepest essential hunger is for life. They put in words an awareness that life is more than being alive. As a self that decides for itself what it wants and needs for life, the psalmist prays for what it wants and needs for life as a physical, social, and religious being. In the anxiety that arises in a self over its life the psalmists see body and others and God in terms of the struggle to possess and control life. In their frequent defense and justification of the self who prays, in the absolute categorization of others in terms of the needs of the self, and in their appeal to self-concern as a motivation for God's help, the prayers are the voice of that struggle to own and possess life.

The specific identity and destiny of the psalmists as they pray is "servant of the LORD," the human beings made able by the electing formation of their history to say "my God" to the power and mystery of the universe. They are selves formed by this further creative knowing. At their deepest level the prayers are a giving way of one person to the other. In the prayers God is not just and only the transcendent counterpart to human finitude and fallibility, a power called on to save and serve the miseries of life. The God of the prayers has a name, a person-to-person identity. The "LORD" is a divine self with characteristics of person and work. In the biblical vocabulary "servant" designates one whose identity and doing are determined by belonging to another. The servant is a person whose self is that of another. The praying self is itself in the relation of belonging, depending, and trusting. That is a relationship in which the autonomous knowledge of good and evil is drawn toward the knowledge of the Lord.

So the psalmic prayers are fraught with an eschatological tension. The help the psalmists seek from God is more than relief and rescue from current plights. Their petitions are the voice of an identity not yet complete and a destiny to be fulfilled. The prayers are a litany of a longing to be what the psalmists are: creatures created in the image of God.

JESUS AS CALL AND PROMISE OF
REPRESENTATION AND LIKENESS

In the New Testament Psalm 8 is cited, the term "image of God" reappears, and descriptions of trouble from the psalmic prayers are used to tell the story of one man's tribulation—all this concerning Jesus of Nazareth. In concert these resumptions from the Old Testament set his person in connection with the promise and predicament of the human recounted there and claim him as the realization of the identity and destiny for which humankind was created. The author of Hebrews, after quoting Psalm 8, says that the realization of humankind's destiny to represent and resemble the sovereignty of God in the world is not visible in the world. But, he adds, "We see Jesus . . . ," and he means the crucified and risen Jesus. In his suffering and death Jesus is one with humankind. Through the power of his resurrection he incorporates humankind in his realization of the identity and destiny for which they are created.

In the Gospels the accounts of the suffering and death of Jesus use elements from three of the prayers for help, Psalms 22, 31, and 69.[14] The words and experiences of the psalmists are woven into the fabric of the passion narratives. What the self in the prayers said and suffered become the words and tribulations of Jesus. In this way the Gospels draw a connection not only between the prayers of Jesus and the psalms, but as well between the person of Jesus and the person portrayed in the self-description of the psalms. There is a kind of recapitulation of the psalmic self in the person of Jesus. The result is a mutual twofold identification. Jesus identifies himself as one of "the poor and needy," joins himself to the company of the afflicted, and asserts a solidarity with them. The psalmic prayers, on the other hand, identify Jesus as a self like the psalmists, a mortal, vulnerable in physical, social, and religious being, who cries out for life and asks in prayer that God's will should serve his life. "In the days of his flesh, Jesus offered up prayers and supplications, with loud cries and tears, to him who was able to save him from death," observes the author of Hebrews (5:7).

He is one like the psalmists, but unlike in one radical way that is disclosed in his Gethsemene prayer: "Abba, Father, all things are possible to you; remove this cup from me; yet not what I will, but what you will" (Mark 14:36).[15] In the matter of life, Jesus' reference to his own will is a link to the psalmic identification. But the phrase "not what I will" is not heard in the prayers in the psalms, an unqualified offering of the self of a human to the "thou" of God. "Although he was a Son, he learned obedience through what he suffered; and being made perfect he became the source of eternal salvation to all who obey him" (Heb. 5:8–9). This crucified risen Jesus is a perfected human self whose person opens up a possibility for other humans that the Pauline letters will call "the image of God."

In the letters attributed to Paul the concept of "image" reappears, to be used to speak of the relationship between God and humankind.[16] It is used first of all to speak about who and what Jesus Christ is. Christ is "the image of the invisible God, the first-born of all creation" (Col. 1:15). He renders the invisible God visible in the created world. He as image preceded the existence of all that was created, so that from the beginning he was the destiny given humankind in its creation as image of God. The gospel brings to light the glory of Christ as "image of God" as it reveals him as the manifestation and likeness of God (2 Cor. 4:4).

The second way "image" is used is to speak of the relationship between Christ and those who are being incorporated in him through faith. Christ Jesus so absolutely preempts the role of image of God that the vocation and destiny of human beings can be realized only through a transformation of their existence by his spirit (2 Cor. 3:1–8). Once in a case of misguided interpretation, Paul does call the male "the image and glory of God" (1 Cor. 11:7). So Paul thinks of humankind as image of God in their created identity, but it is an identity that in human historic life has not been actualized. By the transformative power of the gospel human beings are progressively conformed and transformed to the self they are created to become (Rom. 8:29; 1 Cor. 15:49–51; 2 Cor. 3:18), a transformation that is consummated eschatologically. This transformation that is a being conformed to Christ is discussed in terms besides "image," such as old and new man (Col. 3:9; Eph. 4:22–24), and old and new creation (2 Cor. 5:17; Gal. 6:15).

The paradigmatic action that originates the transformation is the crucifixion and resurrection of Jesus (e.g., Rom. 6:11–14). Paul can say of his own self, "I have been crucified with Christ; it is no longer I who live, but Christ who lives in me; and the life I now live in the flesh I live by faith in the Son of God, who loved me and gave himself for me" (Gal. 2:20). Through faith the love and self-giving of the representative and likeness of God begins to reconfigure the self of others in his own image.

The parallel in the Gospels to this taking over the self of the believer by Christ is found in Jesus' way with the disciples. He interrupts their lives with an unconditional call to follow him. His way is to be their way. Following was a giving up of self to Christ that was a form of crucifixion. They were to learn through Jesus that the effort to be the humankind of Genesis 3:2 and so to save their existence as selves is a way of losing the self (Mark 8:34–38, par.). Along with the entire New Testament the Gospels teach that encountering the crucified risen Jesus inaugurates the transforming of the believer's self.

GOD'S *ANTHROPOS* PROJECT

The psalmic prayers read in the context of the related texts that form their canonical environment support a vision of the meaning and worth of the human being. The self whose voice is heard in the prayers confesses a vulnerability and fallibility of life that belong to every mortal. That the afflictions of finitude and failure are held up to God in prayer is a disclosure of the essential neediness of the human condition. To be human is to be a creature whose nature and destiny in life are incomplete apart from God.

The presupposition and past behind the prayers is creation and covenant. Those who pray are first of all "living beings" created to glorify their creator in lives that represent and resemble God, but "all have sinned and come short of the glory of God." They are also those sinners to whom God has irrevocably committed himself in order that by call and commandment they may be drawn to a fulfillment of their created destiny in ministry to all human beings.

The prospect and promise before the prayers is Christ and consummation. Among the company of the called and commanded, one appears who bears the afflictions of mortal living in a life that perfectly represents and resembles the Creator. The Spirit of his offered and resurrected life is power to transform all and each in the whole human race into fulfillment of the destiny for which *anthropos* was created.

The human race and every individual in it are given their meaning and worth by their location within this plan, this economy of God that runs from creation to consummation. The "mystery" of God and God's way with the world is disclosed in it. The story of the world is the story of God's *anthropos* project. God's *anthropos* project is the divine economy through which God is glorified. As one summary of the Christian faith says as introduction, "The chief end of man is to glorify God and enjoy him forever."[17] And Irenaeus of Lyon declares, "The glory of God is a living man and the life of man is the vision of God."[18]

5

The God Who Reigns

The Book of Psalms

The book of Psalms is one of the two Old Testament books with the most quotations and allusions in the New Testament. The other book is Isaiah. The relationship is clear evidence for the importance of the psalms for the writers of the New Testament. But when the quotes and allusions are examined, it is apparent that they are not usually employed to record what these authors believed about God. Their theology, in the specific sense of that term, seems to be assumed.

THE PSALMS AS THEOLOGICAL PROLEGOMENA

When the quotations and allusions are ordered according to the purpose of their use, the majority fall into two groups. The first is christological—the use of psalmic material to disclose, interpret, and illuminate the person, work, and fate of Jesus as God's Messiah. Obvious illustrations are the citation of Psalm 2:7 at Jesus' baptism (Matt. 3:17; par.), Psalm 22:18 in the Passover narrative (Matt. 27:35; par.), and Psalm 110:4 in the pastoral discourse of Hebrews (Heb. 5:6, 10; 6:20; 7:11, 15, 21). The second group is anthropological in function. Descriptions of the enemy and the wicked in the psalms are used to characterize the fallibility and finitude of the human condition in the human relation to God. Examples are Psalm 5:9 in Romans 3:13; Psalm 94:11 in 1 Corinthians 3:20; and Psalm 34:12–16 in 1 Peter 3:10–12.

What these groupings (along with other less frequent uses of psalmic material) show is that quotations and allusions are not the best guide to the substance and importance of the knowledge of God in the psalms for the New Testament. The psalms, however, contain more direct statements about God than any other book in the two testaments of the Christian canon. God is described and evoked in the hymns, prayers, and instructional poetry of the psalms by testimony to what God has done and typically does and by assertions of the features of God's character. The works of God and the attributes of God are the constant agenda of the psalms. There is a scattered use of the psalmic theological material in the New Testament. Paul cites "The earth is the LORD's and all that is in it" (Ps. 24:1) in his instruction to the Corinthians about dietary practices (1 Cor. 10:26). The call to "taste and see that the LORD is good" (Ps. 34:8) is echoed in the exhortation in 1 Peter 2:3. In Revelation 15:4, "All the nations you have made shall come and bow down before thee" (Ps. 86:9) is read as eschatological prophecy. The declaration, "The LORD is just in all his ways, and kind in all his doings" (Ps. 145:17), is repeated in the heavenly praise around the divine throne in Revelation 15:3.

These examples suggest that the identity and character and conduct of God did not need to be a primary agenda for the writers of the New Testament. The knowledge of God is assumed. They appealed to the book of Psalms and other Old Testament books as a source for the knowledge of God when the need arose in addressing the concerns of Christology, soteriology, and ecclesiology. Otherwise they assumed and read the psalms as authoritative witness to God.

In the matter of the relation between the witness to God in the book of Psalms and the theology of the New Testament, the project must be oriented by the New Testament to discern what is assumed. What elements of the psalms' view of God are necessary and significant for the New Testament, granted that a certain amount of rereading in the light of the developing Christology of the Christian community takes place? The following points only to some of the underground relationships.

"THE LORD IS GOD"

The first and indispensable statement about God in the psalms must be a sentence in which God is the predicate instead of the subject. The term "god" is a class noun. In the language of biblical and contemporary times it can refer to any being reckoned to belong to the class it designates. *Elohim* in the Hebrew Bible is used for any deity or as a plural for deities in general. In the book of Psalms, as in the entire Old Testament, the ambiguity is dealt with by the use of a name. The name is used in two ways: first, to establish the identity of the god to whom praise and prayer is offered and, second, to claim the noun "god" exclusively for the name.

The basic and indispensable sentence is "The LORD is God" (Ps. 100:3). The subject of the sentence is the name YHWH. In the history of the Hebrew text, the consonants of the name, out of reverence, were vocalized as *Adonai* (Lord), and this title itself functioned as a name. The sentence says who God is and who is God. Its purpose is to identify the God who is the theological subject of the psalms and to claim the predicate of the sentence exclusively for the one identified in the subject of the sentence. The effect of the claim is that the noun "god" also comes to be used as an identifying name, the practice found in the group of psalms called Elohist psalms, where "God" predominates as the name, rather than "LORD" (Pss. 42–83).

The proper name YHWH identifies the God who is known in Israel through his works and words. For the writers of the New Testament, God is the One known through Scriptures, the Torah and Prophets and Writings. The works and words of the God of Israel so much constitute the knowledge of God and his identity that the name itself becomes a theologumenon. In Psalms, to pray is to "call on the name of the LORD" and to praise is to "praise the name of the LORD."

In the psalms, all the elements of the faith and language that know and say who God is are assembled in poetry of praise, prayer, and instruction. The psalms in the context of the other Hebrew Scriptures are the indispensable prolegomena to the meaning of "God" in the New Testament. It is this prolegomena that makes it possible and meaningful to say, "he is one, and besides him there is no other" (Mark 12:32; cf. Rom. 3:30).

"THE LORD REIGNS"

The New Testament opens with Jesus' proclamation of the kingdom of God. The theme is expounded and elaborated in his teaching and career. At the conclusion of the New Testament, the book of Revelation opens up the vision of the One whose name is "King of kings and Lord of lords" (Rev. 19:16). The hymns and prayers in the Psalter show how theologically comprehensive and significant the theme is. In the psalms, the organizing theological metaphor is the reign of God. God's relation to all dimensions and aspects of reality is thought of and spoken about as a sovereignty.

In the focal panel of the arrangement of the book of Psalms there is a group of hymns whose theme is "*YHWH malak*" (Pss. 93–100). The sentence is both proclamation and confession of faith. It can be translated as a nominal sentence, "The LORD is king" (NRSV), or verbal, "The LORD reigns" (RSV). The verbal reading brings out better the dynamic active sense intended by the affirmation. The reign of the Lord God is more an activity than an office. It is constituted by what the Lord has done, is doing, and will do. So the language about the Lord's reign in the psalms allows one to think of it as something accomplished and established, something that occurs in specific events, and something expected.

The Lord's active role is the effective power in shaping the two constitutive spheres of reality. God's power is at work in the very existence of the world and in what happens in the world. The Lord reigns in creation and in history. There are psalms that deal with the two spheres separately. Psalms 29 and 93 concentrate on the exercise of the Lord's royal power to establish the earth in the midst of the chaotic and uncreated floods. Psalms 47 and 98 focus on God's way with the nations and peoples of the world and portray the salvation history of the people of God as the manifestation of God's reign in the same world of nations. But the two are coherent and continuous exercises of the same power and purpose, and can be spoken about in the synonymity in which they belong in a proclamation made universally: "Say among the nations, 'The LORD is king! The world is established, it shall never be moved; he will judge the peoples with equity'" (Ps. 96:10). What the Lord has begun in the creation of the world is being enacted and completed among the peoples of the earth. The realization of the Lord's reign is the theme of all reality.

The hymns and prayers and instructional poetry of the Psalter do not, of course, present a systematic account of the reign of the Lord. But this poetry is based on and reflects a theology of God's conduct and character that is foundational for the New Testament. As creator, the Lord is sovereign over all peoples and every person in the world, and all owe the Lord fealty and depend on him for life. The Lord is working in the history of his people. He has claimed them to reveal and establish his reign in the world over the nations and their gods. The Lord is shepherd (a royal metaphor) of his flock and every person in it. He has designated one person as his anointed to play a special role in his relation to his people and especially the nations. As creator, the Lord has manifested himself as "God of glory." In his dealing with his people he has disclosed his holiness (Ps. 9:8), his righteousness and justice (Ps. 97:2), his steadfast love and faithfulness (Ps. 98:3), and his way of combining forgiveness with rebuke (Ps. 99:8).

THE EARTH IS THE LORD'S

In the teaching of Jesus, God is represented as creator, and human beings are regarded first of all as God's creatures. God is "Father, Lord of Heaven and earth" (Matt. 11:25), who "makes his sun rise on the evil and on the good, and sends rain on the righteous and on the unrighteous" (Matt. 5:45), and knows and provides for all human needs (Matt. 6:25). For Paul, "there is one God, the Father, from whom are all things and for whom we exist" (1 Cor. 8:6). In believing and deciding, it is fundamental that "the earth and its fullness are the Lord's" (1 Cor. 10:26, quoting Ps. 24:1).

This confidence that all that exists is the creation of the Lord God and that the identity of human beings as his creations is the truth about their existence and conduct assumes the Old Testament. The Psalms are in this matter the canonical correlate of Genesis 1–2. In what some psalms say and in the very way the book as a whole is arranged, God is viewed in his relation to humans as first of all their creator. God's work in the salvation history of his people is put after and in continuity with the creation work. In this respect, the psalms are open to a reading that includes the way of God with the peoples of the world as coherent with his way with the people of Israel.

The psalms are insistent and consistent in holding the identity of the Lord as creator together with the status of human beings as his creation, who in their createdness are dependent on God and responsible to him. Psalm 8 advocates a theocentric view of the universe and an anthropocentric view of God's purpose in it. The One whose glory is set in the heavens is nonetheless concerned specifically with humankind and has given humans a role in relation to the other creatures that is analogous to God's relation to the universe. Yet, as Psalm 104 says, human beings remain one of the creatures incorporated into the ecology of earth and dependent on God for the gift and maintenance of their life. All is and remains the work of the Lord.

The Lord is not only sovereign over human beings because they and the earth in which they live belong to him as creator (Ps. 24:1–2), but humans individually are bound to him in an intimate and personal way. God "fashions the hearts of them all, and observes all their deeds" (Ps. 33:15). Psalm 139 describes how each person in what one does and thinks and where one goes is "known" by the Lord in a way that includes even the formation of the person in the womb.

The Lord's work as creator establishes the obligation and accountability of all and each to him. Because he spoke and the world came to be, all who live in the earth should fear him (Ps. 33:89). Psalm 24 joins the accountability of humans for their conduct to the praise of the Creator. Psalm 19 even connects the benefits of the instruction of the Lord to the glorious perfections of creation, and the psalmist of Psalm 119 prays that the God who made and fashioned him would give him understanding to "learn your commandments" (Ps. 119:73), another indication that in the psalmic tradition the Torah is being integrated with creation as well as salvation theology.

The way that the two works of God, creation and redemption, are being integrated into one continuous story is evident in all the psalms that recite God's work as creator and God's action in Israel's career as an unbroken sequence (Pss. 135; 136; 146; 147; 148). How harmoniously the two have interpenetrated each other is clear in such a couplet as:

> The LORD is gracious and merciful,
>   slow to anger and abounding in steadfast love.
> The LORD is good to all,
>   and his compassion is over all that he has made.
>   (Ps. 145:8–9)

"SO GREAT IS THY STEADFAST LOVE"

The conviction that God can be trusted pervades and underlies what is said in the New Testament. One can trust oneself and one's destiny to God, no matter what one's need or condition. "Your Father is merciful," says Jesus, even "kind to the ungrateful and the wicked" (Luke 6:35–36). What is said about God in the psalms draws a portrait of a God who is above all else to be trusted. A rich vocabulary of typical actions, attributes, and metaphors is employed to evoke the character of the God to whom the psalmist can say, "O my God, in you I trust" (Ps. 25:2).

The psalms describe how the Lord acts and may be expected to act. The Lord's greatness lies in the fact that he "delights in the welfare [*shalom*] of his servant" (Ps. 35:27). He "redeems the life of his servants; none of those who take refuge in him will be condemned" (Ps. 34:22). He is a righteous judge who does not delight in wickedness. "He judges the world with righteousness, he judges the people with equity," and so is "a stronghold for the oppressed" (Ps. 9:8–9). He is the salvation and trust of all who rely on him.

The psalms contain a catalogue of characteristics to concretize the knowledge of God. The Lord is holy, glorious, and mighty, so he is able to be trustworthy. He is just and righteous, good and faithful, so his character justifies trust. He is gracious, compassionate, and forgiving, so all may trust themselves to him. "His steadfast love endures forever," a refrain that tells the central truth about the Lord (see Ps. 136).

Metaphors are used to unite the conceptual and the experiential in the knowledge of the faithful God. The Lord is rock, refuge, fortress, strength and shield, shepherd, light, guide to right paths—all images that invite trust.

Some psalms seem composed to draw a verbal portrait of this faithful God. Psalm 103 is an example. It begins with a recital of the ways of the Lord with those who fear him: forgiving, healing, redeeming, ennobling, fulfilling, renewing. For the oppressed he works vindication. To the sinner he shows compassion. To mortals whose destiny is dust he gives his everlasting steadfast love. So the human condition of vulnerability, fallibility, and mortality is countered and resolved in the mercy and grace of the Lord. Psalm 25 is another example. It opens with an assertion of trust in God and then moves into a declaration of the faith that grounds the trust. The Lord is the God of salvation.

His mercy and steadfast love have always been there. Indeed, the Lord's faithfulness in steadfast love is the path both the humble and sinner may walk. To those who fear him, he grants his friendship and reveals his covenant.

The psalmic theology of the faithful God is epitomized in a beatitude: "Happy [are those] who [make] the LORD [their] trust" (Ps. 40:4).

"HE DELIVERS THE NEEDY WHEN THEY CALL"

In the entire New Testament there is an assumption that God is disposed toward those who know their dependence on him and against those who undertake to be autonomous. This theological view is expressed in Jesus' beatitudes that affirm the poor in spirit, those who mourn, the meek, and those who hunger and thirst for righteousness (Matt. 5:3–6). It lies behind his instruction to the disciples "about their need to pray always and not to lose heart" (Luke 18:1). The Psalms contain a virtual library of prayers that are the voice of those who know their neediness.

These prayers by their number and passionate eloquence represent the conviction that prayer is the best confession of the faithfulness of God and the essential response of trust in God. The Lord is in his very identity "you who answer prayer" (Ps. 65:2). There is a congruence between true prayer and the being of God.

> The LORD is near to all who call on him,
>   to all who call on him in truth.
> He fulfills the desire of all who fear him;
>   he also hears their cry, and saves them.
>   (Ps. 145:18–19)

To denote those whose prayers are "in truth," the psalms use a vocabulary of dependency. "O LORD, you will hear the desire of the meek; . . . you will incline your ear to do justice for the orphan and the oppressed" (Ps. 10:17–18). "This poor soul cried, and was heard by the LORD" (Ps. 34:6). "You deliver the weak from those too strong for them, the weak and needy from those who despoil them" (Ps. 35:10). "The meek shall inherit the land" (Ps. 37:11). "For he delivers the needy when they call, the poor and those who have no helper" (Ps. 72:12). In English translations, the vocabulary can appear in different words: not only "poor," "weak," "meek," and "needy" but also "lowly" and "humble." Social categories such as "widow and orphan" and "oppressed" are used to the same purpose. The intention of this various vocabulary is always theological, to represent those who by condition, self-understanding, and stance trust themselves to God. The way in which the vocabulary of righteous/wicked is paired with the language of dependence indicates that these terms are more religious than moral. Trust is the first order of righteousness. Autonomous strength, boasting, and self-assertion are habits of wickedness.

The coherence of theology and prayer in these prayer-psalms is evident in passages such as the first seven verses of Psalm 86, in which a sequence of petitions is each supported by a grounding clause. The first is "Incline your ear, O LORD, and answer me, for I am poor and needy." The supporting clauses are statements about the dependency of the psalmist on the responsiveness of God, alternated so as to show the inner coherence of the two. The self-designation of "poor and needy" is paralleled in subsequent lines by assertions of devotion and trust and penitent prayer to show that the neediness of the psalmist is real in his trust and cry.

"YOU ARE MY SON"

The baptismal word said from heaven to Jesus was the inaugural declaration from the Second Psalm: "You are my Son." In the New Testament, the significance of this revelatory announcement primarily concerns the office and role of Jesus. Its portent is christological. But in the case of this sentence, the one who speaks is as important as the one addressed. The declaration has immense theological weight. It discloses God as one who can have and does have and does acknowledge such an intimate and indissoluble relation with a human person. The bare fact of the declaration raises the question about the possibility and purpose in God that informs the sentence. It is the psalms first of all that witness to the God who so binds himself to a person.

The background and origin of God's unique relation to a particular person lies in the Lord's election of David. His relation to David was itself a manifestation of the Lord's sovereignty. In an exercise of his free initiative, the Lord chose David from among the people. He "found" him and anointed him and gave him an identity and dependency expressed in the cry "You are my Father, my God, and the Rock of my salvation" (Ps. 89:26). By the election of David, the Lord disclosed his way and will to vest his reign in the mortality of a man. "I have set my king on Zion, my holy hill" (Ps. 2:6). In the midst of human history, God wills to have a place and a person to reveal and enact his role. The reign of the Lord was identified with him and he with that reign.

In messiah David, the Lord's reign was personified and represented. The messiah is God's representative and agent in dealing with the people of the Lord (Ps. 78:67–72). In their midst he stands for and administers the Lord's justice and righteousness (Pss. 72:1–2; 45:6–7). His strength will be the protection of the Lord's people (Ps. 20:6–9). Through him the Lord will bless his people (Ps. 72:15–17). The messiah is also God's regent in dealing with the nations and peoples of the world. Because the Lord rules over all, the role of his messiah concerns all the world and its peoples. He receives power and authority over the rulers of the earth as the Lord's royal grant (Ps. 2:7–12). His strength and invincibility are an aspect of the power of God (Pss. 18:31–58; 20; 21:8–12). In his exercise of kingship, he will extend the claim of the Lord's kingship over all nations (Ps. 110).

Because of the symmetry between the reign of God and the rule of David, the relationship is indissoluble. By divine sworn covenant the regal office is guaranteed. It is established forever with David and his descendants. So the fate of the representative role vested in the Davidic line places the faithfulness of the Lord in question (Ps. 89:1–18). Indeed, the Lord's deliverance of the anointed from the power of death is a revelation of God's faithfulness to his steadfast love (Ps. 18:1–19, 50). It is through God's salvation of the messiah that the purpose of God in the messiah's kingship is realized (Ps. 18:43–48).

That God's king should reach the fulfillment of his rule in his salvation from death opens up the great mystery about God's way with the Davidic messiah in the Psalms. Because most of the prayers for help in the Psalter are introduced in the voice of David, two strange things are to be noted about this figure who personifies the rule of God. First, in these prayers this agent of God's power discloses that he is one of and one with the lowly, poor, weak, meek, and humble, whose only strength is their trust in God. He is the afflicted righteous one, the brokenhearted and crushed in spirit (Ps. 34:15–18) who prays, "O God, be merciful to me, for in you my soul takes refuge" (Ps. 57:1). Second, the psalmic David can even become the rejected one whose humiliation and degradation contradicts and calls into question God's faithfulness. Indeed, the shame and death of the messiah appears to be the work of God himself (Ps. 89:38–51, especially 43–45). The messiah can cry out, "My God, my God, why have you forsaken me?" (Mark 15:34, quoting Ps. 22:1). And yet it is in and through the messiah's salvation from the powers of death itself that the lowly are given hope, the people of the Lord renewed, and the reign of the Lord is revealed to the world (Pss. 22; 64; 116; 118). Through God's way with the Davidic messiah it begins to become clear that the Lord is a god whose power is made perfect in weakness (2 Cor. 2:8).

CONCLUSION

These are some of the topics and themes that display the significant way in which the psalms form the theological background of the New Testament writings. The relationship between the two is so close and complex that it cannot be reduced finally to a list of topics. The themes embedded in the psalms are in a larger sphere of language used to praise and pray and proclaim God. It is not claiming too much to say that this larger world of language is also the home of the theological language of the New Testament, and thus that the Psalms could be taken up as the direct praise and prayer of the early church. It is the reason the Psalms have often been bound in a volume with the New Testament, as though the Old Testament book belonged in a special way also to the second part of the Christian canon. The author of this article would like to believe that there is in the commonality and coherence of Psalms and New Testament a kind of analogy for the relationship of friendship and endeavor he shares with the one whom this volume honors [Paul J. Achtemeier].

Select Bibliography

Anderson, Bernhard W. *Contours of Old Testament Theology*. Minneapolis: Augsburg Fortress, 1999.

Brueggemann, Walter. *The Message of the Psalms*. Minneapolis: Augsburg, 1984.

———. *The Psalms and the Life of Faith*. Minneapolis: Augsburg Fortress, 1995.

Holladay, William L. *The Psalms through Three Thousand Years*. Minneapolis: Fortress, 1993.

Kraus, Hans-Joachim. *Theology of the Psalms*. Minneapolis: Augsburg, 1986.

Mays, James L. *The Lord Reigns: A Theological Handbook to the Psalms*. Louisville, KY: John Knox, 1994.

———. *Psalms*. Interpretation: A Bible Commentary for Teaching and Preaching. Louisville, KY: John Knox, 1994.

McCann, J. Clinton, Jr. *A Theological Introduction to the Book of Psalms*. Nashville: Abingdon, 1993.

Miller, Patrick D. *Interpreting the Psalms*. Philadelphia: Fortress, 1986.

———. *They Cried to the Lord: The Form and Theology of Biblical Prayer*. Minneapolis: Augsburg Fortress, 1994.

Rad, Gerhard von. *Old Testament Theology*. 2 vols. New York: Harper & Row, 1962, 1965.

Westermann, Claus. *Praise and Lament in the Psalms*. Atlanta: John Knox, 1981.

6

The Question of Context
in Psalm Interpretation

Is it possible and useful to read a psalm as part of the book of Psalms, to understand it under the directives furnished by the book as a whole, to interpret its language by the context established by the piety and thinking inferred from the psalms in the book in their relation to each other? Or, to put it another way, can the mentality that turned the collection of cultic pieces into literature be educed in sufficient specificity to provide a guide to the way the psalms were being understood and composed, a kind of *geistige Heimat* of the Psalter in its final stage of formation?

The possibility of deriving a context for interpretation from the book is not raised as a substitute for the dominant approaches in current psalms study. In the standard commentaries and introductions, psalms are taken up individually and identified as an instance of a genre, and/or as agenda for ritual performance, or as artifacts of Israel's religious history in the context of the ancient Near East. The context for construal is an ideal genre and its proposed history, an inferred festival or ritual occasion, or the ancient Near Eastern history of religion. These approaches have been enormously clarifying and productive. It will be impossible to develop a description of the character of the psalms apart from what has been learned through them.

Of course, the difficulties that arise in giving psalms interpretive identity and context are well known—the tension between the actuality of so many psalms and the ideal genre to which they are assigned, the unresolved questions of cultic history, the perplexing problem of the identity of the individual, the effect on meaning of moving traditional forms and words into quite different periods of religious history, and the extent of redaction in the Psalter. All reckon with the fact that the Psalter is the result of a long history. As the career of Israel passed through dramatic changes, the givens of the settings of earlier psalms change. Traditional patterns and vocabularies took on modified significance and roles. Older psalms were reinterpreted to fit new conditions, and new psalms were written in continuity with classic conventions but expressed the needs and thoughts of later times. Because of the importance of this history for the actuality of its outcome, it seems an anomaly that the Psalter itself is generally so little considered to be significant as an interpretive context. It represents after all the one given context from which to seek guidance about how the language of particular psalms is to be understood.

There are signs in psalms study that this anomaly is recognized and is being addressed in various ways. Among those that I have found particularly helpful are Gerald Wilson's fresh assault on the question of the ordering of the psalms,[1] Joiachim Becker's study of Israel's rereading and reinterpretation of the psalms,[2] Fritz Stolz's description of what he calls the postcultic milieu in which psalms were composed after the exile,[3] a number of studies of the redaction of individual psalms,[4] and the quite different treatments in the introductions of Brevard Childs and Klaus Seybold.[5] In "The Place of the Torah-Psalms in the Psalter,"[6] I attempted to gain some purchase on the question. That paper sought to discover the relation of Psalms 1, 19, and 119 to the book of Psalms. It concludes that this trio, rather than being an odd addendum, stands in a fabric of relations to other psalms and to the whole that gives insight into the terms in which the whole was read, and for describing the piety that sponsored and was nurtured by the Psalter. Strategic as they are for the problem, these three psalms provide only one entry. The net must be cast more widely.

To what kind of data should one look to derive a picture of a context for reading psalms as part of the book? The Psalter seems so patently a collection that the task is discouraging. The framework and integrating redaction to be found in books like Genesis or Judges are not evident in the Psalter. The problem is more like that of a book like Amos, where one deals with an assembly of units. Yet in contrast to Amos, the Psalter seems to contain quite individual and distinct pieces whose relation to each other is not a feature of their being in the book, but rather of sharing a type or function.

I want to propose five kinds of data that can be used to construct a description of the understanding, mentality, and piety that led to and used the book of Psalms. For each kind of data, I point to a few illustrations of what is in mind. I realize that by referring briefly to a selection of psalms whose character I judge to be illustrative, I am begging all sorts of exegetical questions. The illustrations are to be taken simply as pointers to make clear what is in mind and as a way of making the question more specific for the respondents of this essay.

AN INTERPRETIVE ORDERING
OF THE PSALMS

This is the first and obvious consideration that comes to mind, since it is a matter of the book as a whole. Because of the way the book was built, it may not be possible to account for the location and contiguous relations of every psalm in terms of an intentional scheme, but overarching and organizing patterns that point to what the arrangers had in mind have been identified.

The Psalter has an introduction. Psalms 1 and 2 together elevate the paired topics of Torah and kingship of the Lord. This introduction opens a book which with its five sections is itself a kind of Torah. It introduces themes that occupy much of the book—the questions of how individual life and historical destiny are to turn out, the polarity of the wicked and righteous, and the polarity of Zion and messiah and people of God versus the nations.

The announcement of Psalm 2 of the authority of the messiah over the nations has a counterpart in Psalm 89 at the end of book 3 in the great lament over the frustration to the promise to the messianic Davidic king. After transitions in 90–92, the hymns of the coming reign of God in 93–100 follow to put the topics in a prophetic-eschatological perspective.

The prayers of David in books 1 and 2, accompanied by the songs of the official singer-guilds, Asaph and Korah, in books 2 and 3 put the authority of these names and traditions they stand for behind the special identity and use of the Psalter.

The attempt to discern and describe the shape of the Psalter, however, does not reach to all the clues provided by individual psalms. Psalmody began in festivals and rituals of Israel during the era of the kingdoms, if not earlier. It reached its culmination in the formation of the Psalter, though, I believe, without losing its life and function as the provision of liturgical resources for the worship, prayer, and meditation of the people. The crucial psalms for our purpose are those whose redaction or composition reflect the process of movement through stages of cultic history toward the formation of the book. What is needed is to look at these psalms with questions about their implications for views of the whole and for the psalms in it. What features can be identified that point to the way in which all the collected psalms are being understood and used? The context sought, then, is not simply a literary entity; it is also the theological-historical perspective of the mentality that led to the book's formation. So I turn to indications of psalmody's movement toward the double identity of liturgy and literature that belongs to the book of Psalms.

A SHIFT IN THE CONCEPTION AND
USE OF THE GENRES

Psalm 30 shows how the shift in the conception and use of genres involves a loosening of the constraints of the genre on function and its employment in literary and figurative ways. Psalm 30 belongs to one of the classic types. It is a song of thanksgiving for an individual, but its title identifies it as a "psalm for the dedication of the Temple." The individual psalm is designated for corporate use; the report of experience in the psalm now refers to the deliverance of the people from exile. This editorial reclassification is not just evidence of the rereading of one psalm. It may be evidence of the way first-person psalms were being used and composed. The individual lament has become, by way of Jeremiah and Deutero-Isaiah, a paradigm for understanding and articulating the congregation's experience.

Psalm 129 is a corporate pilgrimage psalm, composed in the style of the individual's lament and prayer. Whether the final form is the result of redaction, or more likely an original composition, it shows the literary and figurative use being made of the type.

Psalm 51 is composed in the style of an individual's penitential prayer, but it has elements that show its corporate use, and motifs and language that reflect prophetic hope for the regeneration of the people. Its title connects it with a narrative about David and renders his experience a midrashic type for that of the nation.

FROM RITUAL ACCOMPANIMENT
TO INSTRUCTION

Psalm 33 is an example of the move of psalmody from the primary function of accompaniment toward an increasing expansion of the potential for instruction in all types of psalms. Psalm 33 is a hymn composed with a clear intent to instruct. Comparing it with hymns like 29 or 47 discloses the character of the shift. These first two focus attention on a performance in the cult, while in the case of Psalm 33, attention is focused on the performance of the hymn. It has become the cultic event of significance. All psalms have a pedagogical potential because they say things about God, world, and self. The move in some psalms brings that potential into prominence in all the collected psalms.

Psalm 32 is a penitential psalm written to lead and instruct in the practice of penitence.

In Psalm 24, a catechism (vv. 3–6) on qualifications for entering the sanctuary stands between the little hymn (vv. 1–2) and a liturgy of the entrance of the ark into the temple (vv. 7–10). The catechism centers the other two elements on the topic of the moral character of one's relation to the king of the universe. The unity of the text lies in thought rather than an agenda of ritual.

These and other instances of the developing instructional intent suggest that the groups of psalms usually classified as Wisdom and Torah psalms are not a different kind of species from the rest, but stand in continuity with a long and developing tendency.

THE COMBINATION AND CONSOLIDATION OF GENRES, TOPICS, AND MOTIFS

Psalms 19 and 119 are, of course, parade examples. Psalm 19 combines three topics and styles in unity. Psalm 119 is a veritable montage of genres and topics. They are an earnest that combinations of various kinds are pervasive in the Psalter through composition, redaction, and pairing. Psalms 136 and 145 combine the divine work of creation and providence with the works of salvation history in praise of God's marvelous deeds. Psalms 103 and 104 are connected as a pair by the unique incipit, "Bless the LORD, O my soul." The first is a composition on the topic of the Lord's *hesed* in dealing with sinners, and the second is a composition on the topic of God's wisdom in creation and providence in dealing with creatures. The eschatological hymn that concludes Psalm 22 is an ending that raises the import and setting of the preceding individual prayer to a universal level.

PSALMS IN REFERENCE TO BOOKS OF SCRIPTURE

Psalms 105 and 106 are versions of the foundational story of Israel, reflecting its linearized and fixed form. Psalm 136 elaborates its praise of the Creator-Savior by use of Genesis 1:6–9, Exodus 14:13–15, and Numbers 21:17–22. Psalm 118 quotes Exodus 15:14 and Exodus 15:2, and Psalm 103 quotes Exodus 34:8 and Exodus 34:6 to signal its hermeneutical horizon. And, of course, there is the process of attributing psalms to biblical worthies and connecting some with narratives in the books of Samuel.

CONCLUSION

These, then, are kinds of data that are features of psalmody on the way toward the book. The idea is that they could be used to elaborate and fill out the clues gained from looking at the structure of the book. They are part of the literary character of the book because they are in it. They provide a guide to the way other psalms to which they are related in various ways were being understood as the book emerged. The project would be to build up a picture of psalmody, as description of the mentality that created the book, to be used as a heuristic context to suggest questions and possibilities for interpreting the psalms.

When the psalms are examined from this perspective, questions and possibilities do appear which are not visible when the classic genres and the pre-exilic cult are used as the primary and organizing context. Interest is shifted toward rhetorical structures and the intratextual relations of the language of particular psalms with other psalms and with texts in other books of Scripture. Features of the psalm that were anomalies for other contexts find explanation. The horizons for the text are now the great topics and themes and experiences recorded in Scripture.

The question of who says the psalms receives an open and variable answer that corresponds to the way they were being understood and used. Their functions are opened up to a variety of uses for prayer, praise, and study that reflect their role as both liturgy and Scripture.

But is such a project possible? Does it represent a useful third way to go about the critical interpretation of the psalms? Can the character of the book as constituted by such features be described in a way adequate to serve as a context for understanding the collected poems in their identity as a "psalm" and as a guide to the mentality and piety that created and used the Psalter?

7

Calvin's Commentary on the Psalms

The Preface as Introduction

This essay undertakes a look at some features of Calvin's commentary on the psalms from the perspective of contemporary study of the psalms.[1] The undertaking is obviously and admittedly anachronistic. The usual and scholarly way to describe and assess Calvin's interpretation of Scripture is to read it in the context of the traditions and practices of his own times.[2] But I do not have the learning to do that, nor is it the way I have for some years read Calvin's commentary on the psalms. I rather, as surprisingly many still do, consult the commentary as a resource for psalm interpretation today. When one does that, Calvin's work seems in some respects to be at home with the critical exegesis of the modern world. But in other respects, it belongs to another world—or better, a different mentality. An engagement between Calvin's approach and that of current Old Testament study of the psalms is inevitable and is the focus of this paper.

I want to enter the subject by means of the author's preface, over which stands the heading "John Calvin, to the godly and ingenious readers, Greeting." This preface is particularly well known because it contains Calvin's account of an important phase of his life, a quite personal and passionate narrative of the course of his career from student days to his office in Geneva. It is such an important source for Calvin's biography that one suspects the preface is known and used primarily in this way. So much of the preface is about Calvin that it can be understood justifiably as one of the literary conventions of the period, an author's apology and vindication of why and how he came to write the following work. It is that, of course. But my basic thesis is that read only as such, its purpose as introduction to the commentary and the method of its comment will be missed. The preface not only introduces the author; it is a real introduction to the commentary itself.[3]

For that reason, the preface inaugurates the engagement between Calvin's commentary and current psalms study. The preface stands in such contrast to the typical introduction to a critical commentary that its methodological character is easily overlooked. The typical introduction today will offer a detailed description of the book of Psalms in terms of its content and arrangement, a review of the critical problems set by the material for a genetic understanding, an account of hypotheses and approaches to deal with these problems, including the commentator's own conclusions. There is none of this in Calvin's preface. What and whether he thinks about such things must be learned from reading the commentary. Of course, in Calvin's time many problems of psalm interpretation were those of Scripture in general; they were not yet specialized as they are today. And Calvin writes as if there were a general orientation to the problems of Scripture interpretation that his readers already possessed and he did not need to rehearse.

There were nonetheless issues and questions to be settled, and they do come up in the commentary. Calvin's scrupulous attention to the text led him to recognize many of the explanatory problems with which current criticism is occupied. But where current psalms study resorts to the form-critical and cult-functional approaches, Calvin thinks out answers in terms of the traditional scriptural opinion that David wrote most of the psalms, and that it is David's intention and experience that is expressed in them. For instance, Calvin saw clearly the problem of the shift in mood in the prayer-psalms; but where current study attributes the phenomenon to characteristics of a genre, Calvin explained it by the hypothesis that David recorded his prayers long after they were first made (52, 65). From time to time Calvin notes the liturgical character of the psalms, but he makes nothing of this in terms of their history or the history of the book. He simply incorporates the consideration of this other identity along with their role as David's songs (37, 51). He recognized the introductory function of the first psalm and attributed its place to "Ezra or some other person . . . who collected the Psalms into one volume" (1). These few are only illustrations of Calvin's attention to critical problems, but they come up in connection with specific points in the text and are not gathered up in a systematic way in an introduction as a kind of subject themselves.

What Calvin does discuss in his preface as introduction to the commentary are two subjects typically never treated in any significant way in the introductions to modern commentaries. The first is his intended audience, the readers he has in mind in composing the commentary. Calvin makes the (for current biblical scholarship) astonishing recognition of the role that those for whom he interprets play in the creation and framing of his biblical interpretation. His open involvement with his readers is one major reason for the organization, style, and content of the work.

Calvin writes, he says, for "the edification of the Church" (xlix). His purpose is "to open up this treasure [the book of Psalms] for the use of all the people of God" (xlviii). The commentary is not addressed to other scholars, even those of the church. Its agenda is not composed of the questions set by the problematical and hypothetical. For that reason, he says, he "generally abstained from refuting the opinions of others," even though this would impress peers and reviewers (xlix). Nor does he write for an amorphous general public whose interests and presuppositions are unknown. At every point, even in its intensely scholarly moments, the design of his work, its style and content, are shaped by a notion of the congregation.

Where Calvin does describe the psalms, he discusses the material to be interpreted in terms of its usefulness to the reader. Note, not the usefulness of a critical method to explain the psalms, but the usefulness of the psalms. He tells the readers what they may expect from the study and use of the psalms, and it is threefold. Book and commentary instruct in prayer. "A better and more unerring rule for guiding us in this exercise (calling upon God) cannot be found elsewhere than in the Psalms. . . . Those things which serve to teach us the true method of praying aright will be found scattered through the whole of this commentary" (xxvii, xxxviii). Book and commentary instruct in praise. "There is also here prescribed to us an infallible rule for directing us with respect to the right manner of offering to God the sacrifice of praise" (xxxviii). Book and commentary instruct in the conduct of life, for "the Psalms are replete with all the precepts which serve to frame our life to every part of holiness, piety, and righteousness" (xxxix). One notices that in this broad classification of the uses of the Psalter Calvin has marked off the three primary genres of psalmic poetry with which form criticism works: prayers of lament, hymns of praise, and wisdom poetry.

The shape and strategy of comment is determined by his purpose to let the psalms edify the readers in prayer, praise, and conduct. In his only characterization of the form of his comment on the psalms, he calls it "a simple style of preaching" (xlix). The format of the current critical commentary on psalms will be complex. There will be sections in the comment on one psalm dealing with translation; text criticism; literary and genre analysis; the setting of the psalm in society, history, and literature; an explanation of the language; and some kind of conclusion. Calvin's format is threefold. An introductory paragraph gives the reader a summary description of the particular psalm, providing a characterization of the whole, what the particular psalm is and says, as a context for the following exposition of the text. This little introduction generally summarizes the content of the psalm and the way it is arranged. It discusses the author, especially where the psalm is not attributed to David or anyone. A proposal is usually made about the occasion of the psalm's original utterance. Some situation in David's life, known or suggested by the books of Samuel, is the usual option favored. The technical terms in the psalm's super-scription are considered. Where the function of the psalm poses a special prob-lem, its use may be discussed (109). Not infrequently Calvin anticipates the following content by identifying points in the psalm that are crucial or diffi-cult for the practice of faith. In short, it is in these introductory sections that Calvin takes up the questions of who, what, when, where, and why that occupy contemporary criticism, but he does not work with a fixed agenda. Frequently some of these matters are left to the following comment. Which ones are dealt with in the introduction seems to depend on his judgment of what will be help-ful for the readers to know in advance.

The second part of the format is a translation from the Hebrew text. The translation makes it obvious how well Calvin understood the importance of translation as an interpretive act. The nuances observed in its execution and the disquisitions on the choices to be made in moving from source to target language show how thoroughly the translation was grounded in the resources for philological work available at his time. But even when dealing with spe-cialized matters such as comparing the functions of the Hebrew prepositions *le* and *min* (35–36), or working out the semantic value of *hasid* (42–43), Calvin writes with a simplicity and clarity free of technical terms to allow his general readers to follow the argument. In these and other matters that are occasions for scholarly intensity, Calvin does not lose an orientation to his audience. The items chosen for discussion, moreover, are those that affect the meaning of the text used by the readers. Even the agenda of his explanatory comment seems to be set by a concern with the use of the psalm.

The third part of the format is comment on sections of the psalm. The sec-tions, varying from one to four verses, seem to be determined by content and function, though how the divisions are made is not said. The comment regu-larly addresses two general questions: First, how is the text to be understood, and second, how does the text so understood instruct belief and conduct? These two questions are kept quite distinct in the procedure for comment. Typically, questions of explanation will be dealt with first, and then a transi-tion to the second question is made by using rubrics like "from this passage we learn," or "hence we are taught," or "we may draw the general truth," or "let us learn from the example of David."

The distinction between the two questions and the way in which it is drawn and the importance of the relation and the way it is inferred are cru-cial features of Calvin's approach. He viewed the psalms as philological and historical actualities, texts that express the experience and intention of a person in the past. His agenda of explanation grows out of this view and deals with the problems it poses. In this he is quite modern, and his explanatory work can be seen in a direct line of development with a contemporary critical commentary.

But he also views the text as the expression of the intention of the Holy Spirit. The way in which he moves back and forth between the intention for the writer and that of the Holy Spirit shows he does not think that there are two meanings, but that it is the historical linguistic meaning that is inspired. When he draws the lesson of the text, he does so in remarkable consistency with what he has decided the text means historically and linguistically. He gives the plain meaning of the text a role as instruction that is remarkable in the degree to which these Old Testament texts enter into and constitute the substance of Christian doctrine. In his preface, he says of the Psalms, "that here there is nothing wanting which relates to the knowledge of eternal salvation" (xxxix).

But when one asks how the lesson in the text is recognized, how the potential in the text's meaning is identified, and how it is qualified, the role of the doctrine formulated in the *Institutes* as a grid for reading the psalms as Scripture becomes apparent. The interplay between doctrine and text is not subliminal and unconscious; it is open and intentional. Scripture is the source of doctrine, and so doctrinal questions and needs form the agenda of the application. He expounds the psalms as texts that were written to teach the church how to pray, how to praise, and how to live.

In all these ways, Calvin lets his notion of his readers shape and inform the method of the commentary.

The second subject discussed at length in the preface is the author, Calvin himself. Some ten pages are devoted to a narrative of his experience and career (xxxix–xlix). The form that this little autobiography takes and the claims made in it, when laid alongside the comment on particular psalms, show that Calvin understood his own life to be an immensely important component of his interactive approach. The self-understanding laid out here is central to his method of expounding the usefulness of the psalms for his readers, and this is especially the case with the prayer-psalms written in first-person style. Calvin introduces himself as a medium of the relation between psalm-text and his readers.

An important qualification must be added to this broad claim. Calvin does not, of course, regard the role of his career as the indispensable link between psalm and reader. Using a famous phrase, he calls the book of Psalms "an anatomy of all parts of the soul," and explains that "there is not an emotion of which anyone can be conscious that is not represented here as in a mirror" (xxxvii). This notion of the psalm-text as a mirror was important in Calvin's comment; it repeatedly prompts his observations on particular psalms. He believed that what he called "the internal affections of David and others" (xlviii) as depicted in the prayers were continuous and consistent with those of his contemporaries. What form criticism attributes to conventions of expression and structure belonging to cultic literary traditions Calvin locates in the typical patterns of consciousness that he observed in himself and others. In his commentary on Psalm 3, he says, for instance, that it is easy for every one of us "to conjecture from the feelings of nature" what David felt because of Absalom's treachery (27).

But Calvin makes another use of his metaphor of the mirror when he says that in writing the commentary, "it has . . . been a very great advantage to me to behold in him [David] as in a mirror, both the commencement of my calling, and the continued course of my function" (xl). That is, Calvin not only saw the text of the psalms as a representation of the soul of every believer, but he found in David, whose experience and feelings are expressed in them, a reflection of his own conflicted career.

The little autobiography incorporated in the preface has two parts that tell, as Calvin put it, "the commencement of my calling" and "the continued course of my function" (xl). These are the two poles of comparison. Just as David was taken from the sheepfold and elevated to the rank of supreme authority, so God has taken Calvin from his obscure and humble condition and given him the honorable office of a preacher and minister of the gospel. Just as David was driven to the complaints recorded in the psalms by afflictions he had to endure from those who belonged to his own nation and kingdom, so Calvin has suffered the same or similar things from enemies within his own congregation and religious community (xxxix).

Meditation on this correspondence was a source of strength and counsel to Calvin. By it, he said, "I know the more assuredly that whatever that most illustrious king and prophet suffered, was exhibited to me by God as an example for imitation" (xl). "In considering the whole course of David's life, it seemed to me that by his own footsteps he showed me the way, and from this I have experienced no small consolation" (xliv). It was precisely this usefulness of the psalms in understanding and carrying out his vocation that became one of Calvin's most effective hermeneutical tools. It "assisted" him in understanding the psalms and in applying their instruction to present use (xxxix). Because of his own experience, the psalms were not for him "an unknown region" (xlvii).

It is important to note that the David in whom Calvin saw a mirror of his own career is not what would today be called "the historical David." He is not even restricted to the David known specifically through the books of Samuel. The prayers in the psalms were for Calvin so realistically the words of David that each psalm written in first-person style implied its own occasion. Repeatedly Calvin turns away from any anxious discussion about the relation of a particular psalm to the story of David with the judgment that the problem is relatively unimportant (e.g., 37).

The David of Calvin's mirror is a theological rather than a narrative identity. He is a theological type—a called and installed man of God who is opposed and afflicted. It is this typical identity, conceived in a theological rather than a biographical way, that often provides the relation between the psalm and those for whom Calvin interprets. When Calvin is drawing the lesson from a prayer-psalm, he frequently uses a first-person-plural style and speaks of "we" and "us" in the application. The style is a way of including the reader in Calvin's relation to David. They also, in his view, correspond to the type. They too are persons who are called and installed and have a career as the people of God to live out in the face of tribulation and opposition. True, the Psalms are the mirror of the soul in all its emotions. The mirror's frame encompasses us all in our human condition. But squarely in the center of the mirror stands David, and it is the correspondence between David, Calvin, and Christian that lies at the center of Calvin's hermeneutic, especially when he deals with the psalms composed in the first person.

In commenting on particular psalms Calvin does not adduce the correlation between himself and David directly. But beginning with Psalm 2, as Calvin explains and applies the text, he fills out the comment with copious, repeated, passionate discussions of the experience of conflict and how the godly man is to deal with it. He describes all the forms that hostility can take, the various motives that drive it, the many stratagems enmity employs, its many effects on the afflicted, and the diverse temptations and mistakes that beset the saints because of it. If one asks where he learned all this and why he writes about it with such reality and vehemence, the answer is to be found in the preface, where his own experience of constant and bitter opposition is described as though he were living out the afflictions depicted in the psalms.

The psalms, especially the prayers, furnish ample and repeated texts for the topics of afflictions, but Calvin's comment is not fancy playing upon the text. It is life resonating with the text, and always the focus of this hostility and the locus of its experience is the David who, as described in his first appearance in the commentary, "had the testimony of an approving conscience that he had attempted nothing rashly, or acted as ambition and depraved desire impel . . . ; who on the contrary, thoroughly persuaded that he had been made king by divine appointment, when he coveted no such thing, or even thought of it, encouraged himself by strong confidence in God against the whole world" (9). How does Calvin know all this about David's motives and thoughts? Again the preface, with its account of how Calvin came to his office in Geneva, is the answer at hand. If the reader keeps the preface clearly in mind, one will recognize repeated instances of Calvin's use of this hermeneutic to deal with both explanatory and theological problems that the psalms present.

Typically, the lament-psalms feature unnamed enemies as a major element of the trouble described in the psalms. Current exegesis is divided over what to make of these enemies, and contemporary Christian sensibilities are uneasy at calling others enemies, let alone praying against them. David, Calvin points out, "had well-nigh as many enemies as he had subjects" (28), and that took care of the explanatory problem. In dealing with the theological problem, Calvin customarily warns that when we are afflicted by opposition, we must first take it as a divine chastisement to drive us to repentance of our own sinfulness. But having done that, which he assumed David had done in the penitential psalms (27), we are to ask if the enemies in opposing us are also opposing God. David's opponents attack him whom God had made king and messiah. Calvin's foes opposed him in his office as minister of the Word. This is the appropriate theological setting for prayer in the face of enmity. Christians must discern whether the hostility strikes at the identity given them by the election of God.

A number of the individual laments appeal to God on the basis of the righteousness of the one who prays. Calvin deals with this theological problem by the same reasoning. The story of David in the psalms shows that David was slandered and condemned on every side. But David "had the testimony of a good conscience that he had attempted nothing without the call and commandment of God" (38). The righteousness to which he appeals was not with respect to God but the charges of his opponents (84). It is a righteousness that belongs to all the servants of God, who accepts their upright endeavors (64). To be ill spoken of for doing well was an affliction Calvin knew well, and he believed it was "an affliction which daily befalls the saints" (38). The prayers of the righteous instruct the saints to appeal their cause to God in the face of the condemnation of the world.

Clearly, the psalms have shaped and informed Calvin's understanding of himself and career. In turn, his own experience and his reflection on it have prompted and instructed his comment on the psalms. This is so much the case that one has the feeling of reading Calvin's account of himself as much in the comment as in the preface. Here the hermeneutical circle seems almost perfectly closed.

That Calvin should have given his readers and himself such a significant role in his method of interpretation marks his work as precritical in the judgment of current biblical scholarship. The approach of modern critical study is so pledged to an ideal of objectivity and neutrality with respect to the text, and so occupied with a notion of past history as the strange and alien, that Calvin's approach excites suspicion and unease. Suspicion and uneasiness are the appropriate reactions, however. Calvin from his side raises the question of whether critical scholarship is so boring because it either will not admit to an audience or will admit to no audience beyond itself. He would further inquire whether the pages of the typical current commentary on the psalms do not reflect the self-understanding and career of its author as much as his does. What is lacking is a preface that faces these questions.

Interpreting the Psalms

8

What Is a Human Being?

Reflections on Psalm 8

A recent volume on Christian doctrine begins its chapter on "The Human Creature" by quoting Psalm 8. Such use of the psalm is typical. Psalm 8 has an established place in our theological lectionary because it broaches the subject of anthropology. At its center stands the question "What is the human being?" In other eras, Psalm 8 was used in connection with the doctrine of creation because of its overall theme or with Christology because of the way the psalm is cited in the New Testament. But in our time, the phrase that commands attention is the question "What is the human being?"

The affinity of our ears for that question reflects the mentality of the times. "We live," it has been said of our intellectual climate, "in an anthropological era." In 1863, T. H. Huxley wrote, "The question of all questions for humanity, the problem which lies beyond all others and is more interesting than any of them, is that of the determination of man's place in nature and his relation to the cosmos. Whence our race came, what sorts of limits are set to our power over nature and to nature's power over us, to what goal we are striving are the problems which present themselves afresh with undiminished interest to every human being on earth." Huxley's sense of emphasis was prophetic. The century since he wrote has seen a burgeoning of "the man sciences" and a growing readiness on the part of people to be told what it is they really are.

Though the various sciences that study humankind have by no means reached a synthesis and produced a unified science, interest and curiosity have stimulated numerous popular books written to provide a general answer to the question. The currents that run through these books usually flow from sources in the creative work of Darwin, Marx, and Freud, the three figures whose achievements have dominated the discussion in this century. We hear all about us voices that echo, modify, and distort their notions: Human beings are predators whose natural instinct is to kill with a weapon, an animal created by the union of an enlarged brain and a carnivorous way. The sudden combination of one with the other in the course of evolution created not only the human being but also the human predicament. Or human beings are creatures lived by their unconscious. You know yourself only by getting to know your hidden self. You become yourself only by expressing your repressed self. Or, again, human beings are creatures of the society they have created. Only by a revolutionary change of society can they re-create themselves in innocence and freedom.

Implicit in every proposal about humankind is a diagnosis of the human predicament and a doctrine for its salvation. It is difficult to enter a serious discussion with anyone without hearing the overtones of these proposals. The sciences concerned with humankind have by and large preempted the place in general consciousness that was held in previous centuries by metaphysics, a portentous shift for theology and preaching whose effects are all about us. In the culture of the psalmist's era, the dominant question of human consciousness was, Who is God? In our culture, the question, as it has been traditionally phrased is, What is man?

In Psalm 8, the two questions are held together. Because the psalm has a confident answer of faith to the first, it deals with the second in a particular way. In the way the two questions are held together, the psalm offers a direction and structure of reflection about the question of the human being.

Psalm 8 speaks about the human, the species in general, and about God, a particular god. The way in which both subjects are held together furnishes a kind of paradigm that instructs our time as well as that of the psalmist.

I

That Psalm 8 does, in fact, speak about the species in general and is not merely the esoteric language of sectarian experience cogent only for a group of initiates is a claim that has to be validated. Can human beings recognize themselves in this hymn? Is the psalm's question really an inquiry about the data of being human or merely a rhetorical embellishment of the poem? The answer lies in discovering what experience and phenomena are designed with and under the language of the reflection in verses 3–8. This centerpiece of the hymn is composed of three elements arranged about the question: the sight of the vast and marvelous sky at night, astonishment that God pays attention to mortals, and the assertion that God has set *ben-adam* over other creatures. There is no mistaking the vocabulary of faith the psalm uses. It is creation theology in the classic mode and deals with every aspect of reality in terms of that rubric. The poem is informed by the same vision of creator and creation that is set forth more expansively in Genesis 1.

But when the three elements of the psalmist's reflection are considered carefully, it becomes apparent that the first and the third refer to aspects of general human experience; it is, then, also likely this is the case with the third element. Though the psalm in its meditative rumination speaks the language of a specific faith, with and through it the psalm speaks with and for humanity in general.

1. "When I look at your heavens, the work of your fingers, the moon and stars you have made, what is *ben-adam* . . . ?" The psalmist speaks of the staggering contrast between a human and the great bodies, processes, and powers in the world and the cosmos, the comparison between ourselves and all the rest of reality that, when noticed, brings with it an overwhelming sense of insignificance and displacement. And human beings do notice because unlike other animals who live within a habitat, we are open to the world and cosmos. To know our finitude belongs to our nature. The reflections of humankind from earliest times display this awareness.

In the modern era, the experience is not diminished but heightened. Now we understand that the universe is not measured to the smallest degree by the reach of our sight, nor the march of time by the length of our lives. Astronomers and their planetariums show us the minuscule proportions of our solar system. Beyond our cosmos, the universe stretches from galaxy to galaxy through unlimited void until space curves back on itself. Beneath our sight falls away the partially plumbed depths of matter dissolving into molecules, atoms, and electrons until a void is reached in the other direction. Geologists work out cosmic calendars, informing us that if the measurable course of earth's career were reduced to a year, the history of our civilization would occupy only the last minute of that year. Macrocosm and Microcosm, Space and Time. When we see . . . , what is *ben-adam*?

To look is to experience finitude and transience. We exist in a universe that does not notice or care about us. To be human is to be afflicted with the capacity for this subliminal glimpse of the significance of our insignificance, to live constantly on the edge of consternation before the cosmos.

2. "You gave the human being dominion over the works of your hands. All you put under its authority. . . ." This broad claim about the place and power of humankind in the world stands in sharp contrast to the feeling of finitude and frailty. But in spite of the theological style in which the claim is put, it also refers to a component of being human. It belongs to the human identity to create its own world of culture out of the world that is there and constantly to seek to expand its control of the world by extending the limits of its culture.

When the psalm illustrates what has been set under human dominion, it lists other living creatures. In doing so, the psalm reflects the struggle of early humankind in wilderness and jungle—the arduous venture to master the skills of hunting and fishing, to secure a safe territory against claw and fang, to domesticate useful animals. The psalmist spoke out of the experience of ancient times. In the twentieth century, the list would have to be expanded to include the very elements of matter and the forces of nature. With science and technology, we have pushed the boundaries of culture out to the edges of the earth itself. The drive to control the world in which we live has gone so far that other living creatures, the animals of the psalm's list, are no longer a threat but are threatened.

Precisely because this is so, protests have arisen in our era against what is called the anthropocentric fallacy, the presumption that humans are the apex of the world of living creatures and may bend all things to their own will and purpose. The protest takes two forms. The first is the argument that the anthropocentric presumption is an illusion compounded of prejudice and ignorance. Some who are impressed by the work of comparative biology and paleoanthropology in drawing lines of similarity in connection between animals and the human species have concluded that the latter is nothing but an animal and is to be explained by the phylogenetic heritage with which evolution equipped the species. If we are to survive, we must abandon the superstition that we are unique, come to terms with our animal identity, and make the best of it. Surely this argument has its rights against all the dogmatic and fearful resistance to new knowledge and rear-guard skirmishes against evolution. We are organisms, vertebrates, mammals, and primates, and from all these identities our nature is shaped. But the entire cultural history of humankind contradicts the logic of the "nothing-but-ers." We must be warned once again about the inadequacies of answering the question about humankind from the perspective provided by only one way of studying *Homo sapiens.* Somewhere in the Pleistocene period, a creature emerged with imagination and the power to conceptualize, a creature who could to a degree assume responsibility for itself. It achieved a dominance that is quite unique. The record is an essential clue to its identity, an animal, but one that has the capacity to assume authority over its environment.

The other form of protest against anthropocentrism began with the fact of human dominance over nature and argues that we have gone so far in our exploitation and destruction of the ecosphere that the living creatures, dependent as they are on the processes of nature, cannot survive. Humankind itself is in danger. The answer, it is said, is to let nature be, to live in harmony and modesty within the sphere of life. Nature determines value by what it creates. Every living creature is as valuable as humankind. Elephants have their rights. Humankind must learn to live in the great egalitarian democracy of nature. This argument too has its urgent rights against arrogant, greedy despoliation of the environment and raises the inescapable question of whether we really want the kind of world we are making. But the solutions proposed are often tinged with the romanticism of urbanites who have no real experience of nature left to itself and who, in their real desires, have no intention of being left to nature. Humankind, because of its identity, cannot find a way back into a harmonious ecological matrix and live simply in the rhythm and flow of biological processes. Whatever the true story of our origins in natural history, the outcome that we are transcends the animal world; plans and choices must deal with what we are becoming and not what we have been.

The world of nature is in control, but human history and its effects are out of control. The irony of such apocalyptic-sounding statements is the way they point to the power of humankind in that world. All things for good or ill are set under its feet. "The heavens are *Adonai*'s heavens, but the earth he has given to *ben-adam*," says Psalm 115.

3. "What are mortals that you care about them, human beings that you supervise them?" Here we have to raise the question of whether the second element of the meditation also speaks of a feature that belongs to the structure of human identity. It is easy to assume that the psalm here speaks only of Israel's experience with the Lord, but the language of the text insistently points beyond the religion of Israel. "What are mortals, human beings," it asks, "that you, God, turn to them and pay attention to them?" The assumption in the language is that the riddle of human identity is bound up somehow with its being remembered and visited by God. What is there in the phenomenon of the human that corresponds to this being remembered and visited by the divine?

Would it be an answer to say that mortals are incurably religious, that the pervasive presence of religion of some type in the race is the form of an awareness on humanity's part of dependence on and accountability to the divine? We know from their literature that, in other religions of the ancient Near East, people spoke of the remembering and visiting of the gods in whom they believed. Perhaps the answer will hold for primitive and early cultures and for the middle periods of cultural history.

In the modern period, however, broad sectors of humankind have turned away from the religions bequeathed by history and understood that move to be turning away from religion in general. It is widely held in our secular world that relation to God has no valid place in discerning the nature of the human being. But that conclusion depends on whether, with the denial of traditional religion, the questions and questing—the impulses and needs that were expressed in the religious experience—have vanished.

Because religion is generally considered to be a different realm of knowledge from science, it is usually left out of consideration by the sciences that study the human. But there are impressive claims that the question and quest inherent in religion are essential to the human phenomenon. Sociologist Daniel Bell argues that religion "is a constitutive aspect of human experience because it is a response to the existential predicaments which are the *ricorsi* of human culture." Loren Eiseley marshals the data of anthropology to characterize the human as distinctive in its capacity to transcend itself, a creature who cannot live by instinct but is compelled by a hunger for meanings that come from outside as messages. Novelist Walker Percy (and why should a novelist like Percy know less about the human reality than a psychologist?) in novels and essays attacks the incoherence of attempts to define the human without considering the phenomena of self and soul.

What is this being that longs so much to believe and belong that it gives itself over even to persons and powers who betray and destroy? This form of the question has not been invalidated. Every general book on anthropology that takes up the question in its broadest sense seems to pursue it and inevitably to slide into speculations and statements about faith and fealty that will save humankind from that betrayal and destruction.

So the psalmist does speak of the human species in its frailty and finitude, in its power and purpose to control its world, and in its sense of dependence and destiny. The danger of vigorous theology does not arise from what is known about humankind in our era but rather from the failure to look hard and long and whole.

II

And yet, though the psalm speaks of the species as a whole, it is the particular person of faith who speaks. The poet who celebrates the glory of God in creation is unmistakably a member of the congregation of Israel. God is addressed by the personal name "YHWH," given to Israel as a sign and seal of their relation to God. The poet's experiences of God's remembering and visiting have come as the benefits of incorporation in a people chosen to live out a history whose subject and sovereign was Adonai. The antecedent of the pronoun in "the Lord our God" is the worshiping and believing community called forth by promise, shaped by covenant, and led by hope made known in the Word of the Lord. What the psalmist sees is humankind and world, but both are seen in the vision of faith in the Lord, maker of heaven and earth. The psalm's language contains and converts what is seen into the praise of God. The psalm is itself testimony to the possibility and promise that humankind can know itself and the universe with joy and trust through the knowledge of God.

1. The psalm converts consternation before the chaos into the celebration of creation. Frailty and finitude in the vastness of space and time, yes, but not with an apprehensive sense of being displaced and lost. "The heavens are your heavens, moon and stars are your making." Infinitesimal mortal speaks dia-

logue into the infinite void of the universe, dialogue that is possible because of the faith that God transcends and grounds all that is.

At our modern distance from the ancient world of the psalm, we are inclined to think that it was easy for them to view the heavens with such confidence. The psalm was written when things were simpler, when it was possible to personalize the cosmic environment, when the world was still understood mythologically. They did not know what we know. That is, of course, a brand of modern arrogance that is ignorant of the ethical, intellectual, and spiritual struggle behind the psalm. For millennia, humankind had regarded the celestial bodies as deities and their courses as the source of arbitrary powers that fated and fragmented human existence. To be able to think of sun and moon and stars as creation, as fascinating reasons to wonder but not to be afraid, and to conceive of the universe as centered in one God was an awesome achievement. Indeed, it is the foundation of the confidence on which our modern openness to the universe and the science that emerged from it are based. The problem of saying "your galaxies and your electrons" lies not in what we know, but in whom we trust. If we are to sing at all in the midst of the universe, it will take the form of a celebration of creation that breaks out as the gift of faith.

2. The psalm converts humankind's realization that it has capacity to control and dominate other creatures into the recognition and acceptance of a vocation. It interprets the human drive to transform the world into its world as a role for human beings instituted by God and belonging to their identity.

This intention on the part of the psalm will go unrecognized unless the significance of its royal metaphors are grasped. The place of *ben-adam* in the world is portrayed by using the imagery of the coronation of a king. It is important to keep in view the fact that the psalm here speaks of the human species as a corporate whole, not some powerful sector of it, nor some privileged individual within it. *Ben-adam* has been given a rank within the administrative system of God's sovereignty just below that of the divine court, crowned with glory and splendor, and set up as a king over the other creatures. All has been placed, as the royal idiom has it, under his feet. The picture is one familiar in the world of the psalmist, that of the installation of a vassal king by the ruler of an empire as regent over certain territory that belongs to the suzerain. The vassal's authority is delegated; his rule occurs within the reign of his Lord, whose policy guides his decision and whose purpose sets his goals. The dominion here portrayed as the role of human beings is not self-serving justification to use their power against other creatures and creation as though no desire or needs but their own matter. It is instead a critique and conversion of that view, a claim that human dominance is to be undertaken as a vocation whose source and significance lies in the reign of God, maker of heaven and earth, who created all things and found them good.

The royal imagery has another dimension of importance to it. We are likely to think of the Oriental king as a symbol of tyrannical and arbitrary power. But, in fact, from all we know from the literature of the period, the ideal king was one who was expected to rule for the sake of his subjects. Power was given to him to provide protection, administer justice, and plan for the prosperity of his people. This idea is implicit in the images of the psalm. Humankind is called by God to use the power given it in obedience to the reign of God and for the sake of all the other creatures that its power affects.

From the beginning of the ecological movement, some have charged that the biblical view is the culprit whose arrogance authorized the technological spoliation of the natural world. The fault, however, has not lain in the biblical imagery but in the failure of Christendom to understand and heed it. The royalty of humankind has become a tyranny. The summons in the psalm is to a vocation we have only begun to sense dimly, the mastery of the masters by the Sovereign of the universe.

3. The psalm renders the human need to believe and belong into the words of those who know they have been met and claimed. *Ben-adam* is the creature to whom God turns special attention in salvation and judgment, thereby creating a history that is more than the natural history of the other animals, a history that is open to the future, a history that is dialogue with the remembering and visiting God. Because the psalmist has learned to recognize the remembrance and visitation of God in the history of Israel, he perceives its hidden working in the life of all humankind. The special history of Adonai with Israel is a disclosure of the ways of God with all people.

Mortals seek the unity of everything real in order to be certain of the unity of their own existence. The psalmist announces to humankind, there is a center that holds. There is a healing center for mortals torn by the contradictions of frailty and power, of finitude and infinite obligation. The fragmentation of human existence, the incompleteness of our cognition, and our alienation from other beings are overcome and transcended in the poetry of radical monotheism.

For people in modern culture, who live as we live and who think as we think, the glimpse and possibility of such a center of reality is surprising. We live in bits and pieces, as bodies physicians treat, as psyches counselors console and psychiatrists pursue, as workers used by economic systems, as husbands and wives bound in nuclear families, as minds played upon by dazzling and unordered information and ideas. How can we understand ourselves as one and at one with the All?

The impressive work of Ernest Becker, social anthropologist and Pulitzer Prize winner, in search for a unified science of *Homo sapiens* is a symptom. All his career, until his death, Becker sought the wisdom that could come from the convergence of all the sciences concerned with humankind—anthropology, psychiatry, philosophy, and sociology. He believed the human situation to be precarious and threatened; his hope was that through a unified science of humankind, we might come to know ourselves and take ourselves in hand while there is yet time. In a posthumous publication, Becker says, "The most utopian fantasy I know . . . would be one that pictures a world scientific body composed of leading minds, all fields, working under an agreed theory of human unhappiness. They would reveal to mankind the reasons for its self-created unhappiness and self-induced defeat. Then men might struggle even in anguish to come to terms with themselves and their world." But he concluded, "Yet I know that this is a fantasy. . . ." The common ground that would give coherence to what the sciences have learned about humankind has not been gained; convergence has not taken place.

The psalmist would say that the riddle of *ben-adam* is hidden in the mystery of God. Only faith can envision the point of convergence. Humankind recognizes itself fully only in the recognition of the Being from whom all reality arises.

The claim of the psalm is that we can say "human being" only after we have learned to say "God." It is the particular person of faith who learns to say the word in all its profundity and authenticity. The universal is always implicit in the particular in biblical faith. In a literature where it is Israelites in their experience that are usually in view, that may seem somewhat surprising. But it is surprising only to those who have missed the hermeneutical significance of the canonical arrangement that sets Genesis 1–11 at the beginning of the Bible and the Revelation at its conclusion as a way of identifying the scope of the biblical drama. The psalm instructs and enables those who sing it to speak of themselves as human in no more specificity than the actuality of their own humanity and to speak of all others as no less. Only by speaking and thinking in this way is there any hope of answering the question, What is *ben-adam*?

Philosophical anthropologists point out that, historically, human beings have sought their identity by comparing themselves to animals, to others, and to God. Only the second is absent from the psalm. Here the human is not known by comparison to other races, nations, cultures. The omission is not accidental, and its absence must be emphasized. The notion of universal humankind has been around for a long time, but the drift of history does not favor it. Tribalism, nationalism, racism—all the ways of being human in distinction from others and in hostility to others—govern the self-consciousness of the majority of the species. In every crisis of culture and at every transition in history, we have to learn again how to say "human being." By any other language, we do not discover but destroy ourselves. And in that fact alone, the left hand of the God of the universe shepherds us toward the realization of universal *ben-adam*.

Can we also say, softly and modestly, that it is only this particular person of faith who can speak of and proleptically exist as universal *ben-adam*? We are not much moved, we mortals, to imagination and change by generalities and definitions. They come rather with the inspiration that grasps us in quite individual and personal encounters, confrontations that take us out of ourselves and open us to possibilities we had not conceived or wanted. Beyond the unreserved openness with which "human being" is said in Psalm 8 lies the summons to a particular folk to be a peculiar people as a blessing to all the world, lies a vocation to be the Lord's own people as a signal that all the earth belongs to God—and for us there stands a man who in the individuality of his suffering and death stood for all. From such encounters, the idea of humankind becomes a promise and a vocation, a cause to celebrate and sing psalms.

9

Old Testament Psalm, Cry of Jesus, and Christian Prayer

Psalm 22

One of the ways the church has used the Old Testament as its Scripture is as a witness to Christ. Christians have read it to know their Lord better. That is what the writers of the New Testament did, and the church fathers, using several hermeneutical approaches, continued to read the Old Testament christologically.

Modern criticism has placed a question against that familiar hermeneutical habit by insisting on the historical and generic as definitive features of biblical texts. The Old Testament is the literature of the religion of Israel, which knew not Jesus. Its typical function is not oracular revelation about a messianic future, and where it is prophetic, prophecy is more forth-telling than foretelling. Where the values of modern criticism have prevailed, the christological use of the Old Testament has been left to liturgy and sometimes preaching, without exegetical foundation.

Now I do not think we can "go home again." We cannot return to a precritical reading—or go on to a postcritical hermeneutic that forgets in a second naïveté that the historical and generic questions have been asked. They are as native to our consciousness as the allegorical and typological were to other earlier times. But neither can we give up seeking the relation between Old Testament texts and the identification of Jesus as Messiah. We cannot read the texts with the same consciousness of the apostles and fathers, but we can read with the same conviction and basic questions. Precisely our perception of the historical and the generic way helps us to knowledge of the Lord that is appropriate for the theological questions and needs of our own time.

I propose Psalm 22 as a case in point. The choice is, of course, prompted by the New Testament and by liturgical practice. The first line of the psalm is said as prayer by the crucified, dying Jesus in the Gospels of Matthew and Mark. During Holy Week the psalm is traditionally used on Good Friday.

Now, we could read the psalm as the words of Jesus and understand it in light of his suffering. That is what we usually do, and I would insist correctly, in the recreative remembering of liturgy. I want, however, to move in the other direction and ask what is to be learned by understanding his suffering through the language of the psalm. Does it, as Old Testament text, testify to his christological identity?

In seeking an answer to the question, I consider the entire psalm, and indeed the genre of psalms that modern criticism has identified. Jesus, of course, in the cry from the cross says only, "*eloi eloi lama sabachthani*," the opening sentence of Psalm 22. But sometimes brief quotes from the Old Testament are directives to the reader to reflect on the text so identified. I believe that is the case here. The entire psalm is viewed as though it were the libretto for our Lord's dying.

The probability that this is so is supported by the appearance of motifs from Psalm 22 in the passion narrative. When those who crucified Jesus divided his garments among them, casting lots to decide which each should take, verse 18 of the psalm clearly is coming into play: "They divide my garments among them, and for my raiment they cast lots." Those who pass by the cross derided him, wagging their heads, says the Gospel; and in verse 7 of the psalm, we read, "All who see me mock at me, they make mouths at me, they wag their heads." The psalm goes on in verse 8, "He committed his cause to the LORD, let him deliver him; let him rescue him, for he delights in him," an element that also enters into the passion story of the Gospel. And there are other allusions. As one looks at these connections between the Passion story and the psalm, it would appear that the suffering described in the psalm is enacted in the Passion of our Lord.

Lines and motifs from other psalms are used to compose the narrative of the passion, particularly two: Psalm 31 and Psalm 69. For instance, the offer of wine mixed with myrrh and the sponge soaked with vinegar reflects elements of Psalm 69. This further connection between passion story and Psalter leads to a particular type of psalm, the prayer that form criticism calls "the lament of the individual." This compounds rather than relieves the mystery. The lament of the individual is the prayer of the Old Testament par excellence. It is massively present in the Psalter; there are more of them than any other type. Outside the book of Psalms, it is used in narratives and heard from prophets. This means that Jesus speaks on the cross as countless persons have—and as an Old Testament man. The Old Testament lament itself seems to be the context in which this climactic event of the New Testament is to be at least partially understood. Add to that the fact that the lament is not the style of prayer customary for Christians. Its insistent boldness in holding up all of life's worst, with its vehement demands for God's responses, is a devotional strategy that makes us distinctly uneasy. We may read these prayers in our liturgies and in our formal devotions, but they do not seem to come naturally or easily to our lips.

What does it mean that our Lord in his deepest agony prayed as Old Testament men prayed and in a way we do not usually pray?

CHARACTER OF THE LAMENT

A lament is a prayer composed and said to hold up the needs and afflictions of mortal life to God. A lament is, in a word from Psalm 130, a cry from "the depths." The title of the 102nd is virtually a definition of the genre: "A prayer of one afflicted, when he is faint and pours out his plea before the LORD." The lament is the classic form of the appeal to God for deliverance. Their abundance in the Psalter is an eloquent witness of the way in which Old Testament piety bound the tribulations of mortal life to faith in God as savior.

These laments are made up of a consistent list of component elements, which occur in a variety of arrangements. They usually begin with some form of direct address to God, a vocative like "my God." They always contain a complaint, or the lament proper, in which the trouble of the one who prays is described. A specific petition is made for deliverance from the trouble. It is usually accompanied by what are called motive clauses, statements of reasons why the petition should be heard. The laments also include statements of confidence or assurances of being heard, and may conclude with a vow of offering or praise.

Psalm 22 and the other psalms employed in the passion narrative are prayers composed of these typical rubrics. Indeed, in Psalm 22, the typical is raised to such an extravagance and intensity of scope and dimension that it appears to exhaust the possibilities of the typical and bring it to its ultimate statement. The opening vocative begins a prolonged cry to "my God" which grows in urgency through twenty-one poetic lines. The trouble, the occasion for the prayer, is described in the three ways conventional in such laments: in terms of the pray-er's experience of God, of others, and of self. His life is empty; he neither hears the Word nor senses the Presence. He is surrounded by people who mock his suffering, dehumanize him with cruelty, and take bestial forms in their ferocious inhumanity. Anguish of dying and apprehensions of death overwhelm him. Interspersed in the descriptions of troubles are professions of confidence in God who delivered the fathers of his people when they trusted him and who has been his personal God from before his birth throughout his life. Punctuating the whole and carrying its intention is the recurrent plea "Be not far off. . . . Help me."

Just when the alternating combination of these three moods has gone on until its tension is well-nigh unbearable, there is a shift to a stance in apparent contradiction to the preceding prayer. The prayer becomes a vow that the forsaken, rejected, dying one will stand in the midst of his community of faith and testify to a deliverance that will bring forth praise of God from the congregation and give hope to the afflicted. Indeed, his testimony will become a memory, a tradition, everywhere and in all times, which witnesses to the universal dominion of his God and the God of his congregation.

Powerful and exceptional as this psalm is in its particularity, it does not abandon the formulaic and typical characteristics of the lament. Form and context are an inseparable unity. The medium may not be the message absolutely, but the medium is an indispensable dimension of meaning.

If we could find in the particular individuality of the psalm's language some clue to the identity of the one who prays here, that might relieve the importance of the typical in favor of the individual. Whose is this prayer? The attempt in Old Testament study to answer the question has been inconclusive; or to put it more accurately, the search has come upon several possibilities. And several answers, rather than one, must be nearer the truth of the matter. Was the Israelite who wrote this prayer sick, perhaps of leprosy, or judicially or politically persecuted? Is the psalm purely liturgy designed for use by any pious Israelite in desperate trouble to pray for salvation at a sanctuary? Is the one who prays a king, and is that the reason for the importance his person assumes in the prayer in relation to God and foes? And is this king's suffering ritual drama or historical experience? Did the community use this prayer in exilic times and later to give a corporate voice to national tribulation? Does the attribution to David signal that the psalm was understood as an expression of his story, with all that implies for its use?

All of these proposals have been made in Old Testament research. Each one of them has some purchase in the text of the psalm. But its language is too vivid and vague to lend any one of them conclusive support as the only way to understand the psalm. The very typical character of the prayer qualifies its individuality and keeps it plastic to different uses. Surely, this is a text that has had a life of its own. In all probability, it has had a career in which its words served as language for parties and purposes we usually think of as opposites—for individual and community, for citizen and king, for liturgy and narrative tradition, for cultic enactment and eschatological proclamation. Its generic character equips it to bring its individuality to all these parties and purposes as interpretative identity.

From the perspective of the New Testament and the use of the psalm on the cross, this inconclusiveness of research is not liability but asset. When the psalm is used as a libretto by the passion narrative, that is not simply an anachronism or anomaly. It is a release of the hermeneutical potential in the character and career of the psalm. The current flows both ways—from psalm to Jesus and from Jesus to psalm. The psalm brings its interpretative identity to the suffering Jesus. Jesus' passion is a new setting in which the psalm can be understood. It is in the first that the psalm as type and medium of language is at work. It is that on which I will concentrate in pursuit of our question about Christology and prayer.

LAMENT AS A DISCLOSURE OF HUMANITY

Let us begin with the recognition that the voices who speak in laments of the Psalter are human women and men. I suppose the suggestion points to what is so obvious as to appear banal and superfluous. But I intend something that transcends the obvious. The laments are vehicles of expression for universal and essential humanity. Some language isolates those who speak. It divides and separates. It is hardly the language of corporate humanity. Some language is meant to conceal the humanity of a person—hardly the language of essential man. It is the eloquence of suffering, which, finding vocabulary and style and form adequate to give it full voice, comes closest to the language of universal and essential humanity. Here are heard the vulnerability and mortality and anguish and questions that belong to all because they are inherent in the human condition. That is the first thing that is happening in the psalms of lament.

For this reason, it should come as no surprise that such poetry is not peculiar to Israel. Indeed, that would be strange. Instances of the lament with similar components and style appear in the literature of other peoples. People hurt in other cultures, and found words to say so, before Israel existed and alongside Israel when it did exist. The basic form was the creation of others. Israel brought it, as they did with the hymn, to the fullest and finest expression. So, the laments of Israel entered into and gathered up an unlimited community of pain and protest that, wider than the form itself, includes all whose suffering lacked the form and words of eloquence. The whole background of mankind, expressing mortality, echoes in all of them and each of them. The bell for humanity tolls in everyone.

Moreover, in the threefold structure of the complaint, Israel fashioned a descriptive form that encompasses the fundamental dimensions of human consciousness. As we have already noted, the complaint is typically directed toward God (an accusation or complaint against God), toward other people (complaint against an enemy), and toward the lamenter himself. The whole of man's being comes into expression in these three dimensions, for the lamenter is not merely the isolated "I" who is threatened by the power of death experienced in suffering—threatened as well in his standing in the community, that is, what he means to others and what they mean to him—but also threatened is the meaning of his life. That is what the "why" of his complaint against God is all about. The answer to the question of meaning, to the question "why," cannot be provided by the sufferer himself. The question must be directed to the source of life, and only from thence can an answer come. This threefold description of the self is an expression of existence that is simultaneously personal, social, and theological. It is an inclusive assertion provoked by the experience of pain about what it means to be human.

From this perspective, the cry from the cross takes on a significance of incredible breadth. When Jesus begins to sing the lament, he discloses the involvement of his full humanity in the crucifixion. It reveals him as one of us in the most total sense. It is the moment of his profound identification with us—when in his consciousness of himself, of others, and of God, he embraces the actuality of human existence. He is one with essential and universal humankind. It is the truth to which the demonstrative sentence "Here is the man" (John 19:5) points.

LAMENT AS LANGUAGE OF FAITH

A second characteristic of the lament that sheds light on our question is its function as language of faith. Again, this feature seems so obvious, but it is also one that can easily drop from sight in dealing with these peculiar prayers. Their impassioned, impatient rhetoric, so intent on giving vent to the feelings of the one who prays, and so full of the words of forsakenness and helplessness, does not sound like the stance we usually name *faith*. Commentators and interpreters easily slip into talk of despair and dereliction in dealing with them. But in our modern discourse, despair means to be alienated and alone in the universe, to be without hope. The laments, however, desperate in their language at points, are not the poetry of existential alienation.

Psalms like 22, 69, and 31 are in their very function dialogical. Their initial vocatives calling out "O LORD" or "my God" are powerful assertions of the reality of the ultimate Other. Those who pray are lonely, but not alone in the universe. Therefore, though they may be helpless, they are not hopeless. The dialogue can and must occur because God is there, and only from the divine direction can the response come that makes sense and salvation out of the plight. Despair sets in when the dialogue is stilled. But when it occurs, it is the most poignant expression of faith given to the lips of mortals.

E. M. Cioran's book *The Trouble with Being Born* is in a real sense the personal odyssey of one who wants to take up the dialogue and cannot. But it contains a striking aphorism that from the side of sophisticated modern alienation makes the point under discussion: "A cry means something only in a created universe. If there is no creator, what is the good of calling attention to yourself?" Cioran means the aphorism as a statement of his own despair, but it is a true statement. In his longing for the dialogue he cannot resume, he discerns what happens in a lament. It is a way of calling attention to oneself, the ground and goal of which is the assertion of God. It is the language of the martyr par excellence, the one who makes of his sufferings the occasion and means for witness.

In understanding the lament as the language of faith, we must not forget for a moment what the subject of these prayers is. Not the fulfillment, well-being, inspiration, and vindication that our culture identifies with faith and seems to think exhausts its reality. No! The subject of these prayers is the worst of life, the experience of weakness, hostility, pain, and dying. Their very genius is that they resolutely hold all that up to God, insist that it can be borne and transcended only in the divine context. There is in these prayers no embarrassment about the whole range of mortality's travail. Rather, it is believed that it can all be incorporated into God's way with those who cling to him.

Now if this be true of the lament, it becomes clearer why this kind of prayer is the basic stock of the Psalter, and also why our Lord took up one in his final agony. When Jesus cried out, "My God, my God, why have you forsaken me?" it was the climax of his role as witness. He entered into the language of faith that had been prepared in the history of his people for such travail. In the midst of all that argued for the godlessness of the world, he claimed the reality of God. His prayer was a proclamation that the worst—the anguish of the body, the hostility of others, the encroachment of death—are the setting for the dialogue with God at its most intense.

Perhaps this feature is one important reason why these strange prayers maintain a persistent presence in liturgy and devotion. It is not simply because they are in the Bible, or even because they echo at points the language and life of our Lord. They are the place in Scripture and worship where the full agenda of pain finds words to bring its burden into the presence of God. They hold hurting and faith together. The traditional tendency of corporate worship and individual devotion is to concentrate on sinfulness as the one dimension of the human condition put in focus. But the psalms of lament resist the reduction of human need to individual guilt and the recitation of finitude to the confession of sin. Life, along with its joys, is beset by loneliness, disease, hostility, anxiety, bewilderment, anger, hatred, and pain. The laments give all that voice before God. They enable us in our anguish to speak to God as we are, and as we feel.

THE PLACE OF PRAISE IN THE LAMENT

The third characteristic of the lament that bears hermeneutic significance for the cross is the great turn, the surprising shift in mood and intention within the psalm. In many of these prayers, the alternation of complaint and supplication is deserted for another kind of language: that of praise. The laments complete themselves in hymns whose sole subject is God in his powerful mercy. In Psalm 22, the break comes at verse 22 with "I will tell of your name to my brethren; in the midst of the congregation I will praise you."

The praise continues in various idioms for seven verses. The suffering one vows to call his fellow believers to praise the Lord because the Lord has heard his cry. His deliverance will show that God has not despised (as humans do) the afflictions of the afflicted. Others who are afflicted may take hope at his deliverance. Indeed, God's response to his cry of need will be a sign to all throughout the world and until the end of time that dominion belongs to the Lord. His anguished appeal to God has been made an event in the reign of God. His vindication takes on a universal scope and enduring significance that matches the totality and intensity of his passion.

The dimensions of suffering and deliverance described in Psalm 22 are unparalleled in the Psalter. But the shift from plaint to praise is typical. It poses the central mystery of the lament. How is it possible from a human-psychological view for one utterance to combine such irreconcilable opposites? A variety of explanations have been proposed. Perhaps the answer is liturgical. In the interval where the break comes, a prophet or priest pronounces a word of salvation. Perhaps there was a dramatic ritual enactment of the change from tribulation to deliverance that both reflected and promised the recurrent pattern of Israel's experience with God. Some interpret the change as a transition in the mood of the psalmist, a biographical psychological approach. And so on.

But no explanation in terms of the origin of these psalms in the experience of someone who composed them, or in terms of the way they were used in the Old Testament liturgy, really solves the riddle. We are left to ponder the mystery by the silence of history on the question. These prayers with their great turning, their conversion of plaint to praise, are simply given us by the Scripture—given us with their mystery as though in tracking their course across their great divide we would realize its possibility and meaning, or as though the answer might be given us from somewhere else. Both, I think, turn out to be true. But the latter depends on the former.

When we hear Psalm 22 as Jesus' prayer on the cross, the shift from lament to praise becomes a word about the universal saving significance of his passion. The prayer testifies that this prodigious suffering will become the occasion and reason for the joyous celebration of the reign of God. Out of it will come a witness that encourages all who depend on God and sustains all who are afflicted. It will be remembered to the ends of earth and through coming generations. Where the witness is heard, the proud will be humbled; the dying take hope. It will become the proclamation of the righteousness of God. All this, the prayer says in its final words, will come out of the suffering "because God has done it."

Enigmatic sentence! What does it mean? It is a formula that occurs in the Old Testament in a quite specific context and function—always as a testimony that a deliverance from dying (for an individual or the people) is the work of God. It is a revelatory code word from the history of salvation. It says that even the suffering and dying described in the prayer are included in the sphere of God's righteous reign. Nothing that comes to any human being—no tears, no depth, no anguish—is beyond and without the kingdom of God. Even death entered into in dependence on God is gathered up in his purpose. Nothing borne in faith is lost. The blood of the martyrs and the dying of the faithful are incorporated into the righteousness of God. The psalm tells us that the resurrection does not cancel the cross; it validates and reveals it as the central moment of God's reign. The resurrected one is the crucified Jesus. Faith is not relieved of mortality and suffering. Anguish and death in faith are rather trans-figured by their absorption into the coming reign of God.

The Jesus of the gospel has claimed Psalm 22, and its companion psalms, as his. It is ultimately his prayer because his passion enacts, and so fulfills, the dimension and scope of their pattern. As Old Testament prayers, they sketch a transaction between suffering faith and God for which their composers longed and reached. It is a transaction we also long for—and cannot reach on our own. We could never make it across the great shift—apart from hearing his prayer as word to us.

We must hear that word in order to pray these prayers ourselves. Then their pattern begins to conform our praying to his passion. Because they lead us to speak to God both in plea and praise, to pray out of the experience of for-sakenness and grace, we may come upon something about God and ourselves that is hidden in the symbol of the cross.

God is so much a God of blessing and salvation that one must speak of tribu-lation and terror as the absence of God; yet God is so much the God of grace that one can speak to God in the midst of tribulation and terror as the God of salvation. This is the deep radical knowledge of faith that cannot separate God from any experience of life and perseveres in construing all, including life's worst, in terms of a relation to God. It is the expression of such a powerful experience of graciousness that it refuses to see the present apart from God and cannot imagine the future apart from God's salvation.

Paul knew about this when he said, "For I am sure that neither death, nor life, nor angels, nor principalities, nor things present, nor things to come, nor powers, nor height, nor depth, nor anything else in all creation, will be able to separate us from the love of God in Christ Jesus our Lord" (Rom. 8:38–39). Paul knew that there would be depths and death. Faith does not hide from that or decline to speak of it. But he had also learned that these things were not incoherent with the triumph of grace.

Luther learned to see through the apparent contraction. In his exposition on one of these psalms, he calls its mood the "state in which hope despairs, and yet despair hopes at the same time; and all that lives is 'the groaning that cannot be uttered' wherewith the Holy Spirit makes intercession for us, brooding over the waters shrouded in darkness . . . this no one understands who has not tasted it" (Luther's Commentary on Psalm 13).

We are shown who we are when we pray. We are taught our true identity as mortals who stand on the earth and speak to a God who is ours but never owned. Agony and adoration hung together by a cry for life: This is the truth about us as people of faith. The blessedness of this disclosure is that it strips us of all illusions that our faith is a cure, an escape from our trouble, a panacea for the awful anxiety and fear that belong to humanity. We would like to think that we begin with lament and make by faith a perfect transition to praise, leave doubt and fear behind, and emerge in trust and security. Surely faith works. Surely one day we can say, "I believe" without having to cry out, "Lord, help my unbelief."

Nothing in the careers of the prophets or in the letters of the apostles or even in the life of our Lord suggests that it is so. In this world as it is and in this humanity as it is, faith is more likely to bring the tears of a Jeremiah, the stigmata of a Paul, a night in Gethsemane. These psalms are not prayers to be used only on occasions when some trouble makes them appropriate for us as long as this life shall last. The agony and the ecstasy belong together as the secret of our identity. We are simultaneously the anxious, fearful, dying historical person who cannot find God where we want God to be and the elect with a second history, a life hid with Christ in God. "How long, O Lord," we lament into empty spaces. We also say, "You have dealt graciously with me." And all the while we pray for life in our dying, pray because through the gospel we bear already in us a foretaste of life to come.

Jesus began Psalm 22, but he did not make the great turn in words. He died. The psalm was completed in his resurrection when he proclaimed to his community and they to the world that God has not despised the affliction of the afflicted. Forsakenness and deliverance are held together in his death and resurrection. The crucified Jesus is the risen Lord; the risen Lord is the crucified Jesus. His praying has become that word, and in that word we can hold suffering and hope together.

10

A Closer Look

Psalm 23

OUR FAVORITE PSALM

The psalms have the marvelous capacity of becoming the voice of those who read and recite and sing them. In their use the user is drawn into a kind of merging with the psalmist. The experiences and need and faith expressed in the psalm resonate with those who ponder them. The "I" and "we" in the psalm can begin to incorporate the identity of those who take them up. The power to claim the consciousness of those who use them is surely a principal reason why the psalms have played such a constant and important role over the years in the life of Christians.

There is a compelling record of this role in a book written a century ago, *The Psalms in Human Life*. Its author was a British nobleman (Roland E. Prothero, Lord Ernle). What he undertook to show was that from apostolic times important figures in the history of Christianity had used the language of the psalms as their speech in crucial occasions of their lives. In times of stress and of exhaustion they spoke with the words of the psalms. Prothero showed how the Christian story is a history accompanied by an almost liturgical music of voices telling their story in psalmic cadences.

Once, while walking in the Virginia mountains, I came across a small family cemetery. It contained the graves of the family of a doctor who lived and worked in the area in the early 1800s. At the center of the graves a small four-sided obelisk stood with inscriptions on each face. As you walked around, it read, "The Lord is my shepherd"; then, "He restoreth my soul"; and next, "I will fear no evil"; and, finally, "I will dwell in the house of the Lord forever." As I circled and read, the awareness that these sentences were far more than decorative quotes grew. It was as if I were listening to the doctor speaking, using the psalm to witness to his faith to anyone who, like me, chanced to pass by and stopped to read—and listen.

The quoted psalm is, of course, the Twenty-third. Of all the psalms, this is undoubtedly the best known and most loved. It is the one we most easily read and recite, claiming its first-person voice as our own, feeling ourselves the "I" in the psalm. The Twenty-third is used on so many occasions. The common lectionary assigns it appropriately to the Sunday service for the fourth week of Lent, but it is most often said and read in the rites of death, funerals, and memorial services. That gives it especially poignant and emotional associations.

Because that is so, one must hesitate to offer an interpretation of Psalm 23. During a long career of speaking and writing about psalms I have always before now turned away from it. Any interpretation seems presumptuous. The Twenty-third is poetically so precious and so owned by all who know it that it ought not be blurred by the comments and glosses of an interpreter. Why undertake to explain a psalm that in its use so rightly speaks for us and interprets us?

So the following observations are offered modestly and in reverence. They concern three features of the language of the psalm: the predicate of its first sentence, "shepherd"; the verb of the second sentence, "want"; and, finally, the first-person pronoun in all the sentences, "my, I, me."

THE PREDICATE OF THE FIRST SENTENCE: "SHEPHERD"

We deal here, of course, with a metaphor. A metaphor offers us an image of something known to help us know something else better. It says something is what it literally is not so we can imagine better what it is.

"The LORD is my Shepherd." God is equated with a vocation, "shepherd." In Hebrew, the equation is stark. The sentence has only two words (YHWH my-shepherd).

As so often the case with a psalm, the first line says something about the whole. The whole psalm is metaphorical, comprising poetic images. The rest of the psalm unpacks and expounds the initial metaphor.

A shepherd provides for, guides, and protects his flock, and that is what the psalm describes: the providing, guiding, and protecting of the Lord.

So far, so good. That is, if you do not try to outline the psalm into three parts called (1) provide, (2) guide, and (3) protect. There is no set order in the psalm of these three duties of a shepherd. The duties are combined in the psalm's poetic images. Is "lead me beside still waters" guiding or providing or both?

Another problem: the psalm does not keep to images we associate with "shepherd"—for example, "You prepare a table . . . you anoint my head." We are still with functions of provision and protection, but not the way shepherds provide and protect.

The reason for these apparent inconsistencies is that "shepherd" in its use as a metaphor in the ancient Near East and in Israel was a complex, not a simple, metaphor.

In the ancient Near East "shepherd" was a frequent and common image of the relation of a sovereign to his people. In Israel it was a favorite image of YHWH's relation to the covenant community. The "rod and staff" in the psalm are actually the symbolic equipment of a king instead of the tools of a shepherd. To the author of Psalm 23 "shepherd" was royal as well as pastoral. The author was writing of the providing and guiding and protecting by a ruler as well as by a shepherd.

THE VERB OF THE SECOND SENTENCE: "SHALL/DO NOT WANT/LACK"

Actually, the first poetic line has two complete sentences. The second is composed in Hebrew only of a negative particle and verb. The anomaly, and attention-getter, is that the verb is transitive. The verb is supposed to take an object: "I do not want/lack WHAT?"

Is the answer "anything"? Could the psalm possibly say, "I do not want anything?" Who here cannot make up a want list of many items? Sinner that I am, my want list would probably include things I do not need and should not have. Given the human condition it is so easy to confuse "desires" with "needs."

The psalm does not leave us to make up our want list. The missing object of the verb is supplied by the rest of the psalm. When the Lord is your shepherd, you do not lack the nurturing and guiding and protecting of your soul. "The LORD is with you; he restores your soul." The psalm is about the soul-restoring presence of the Lord. Remember the spiritual that goes:

> Sometimes I get discouraged
> And think my work's in vain.
> But then the Holy Spirit
> Restores my soul again.

Note that the psalm does not foster a rosy view of life, a cheap optimism, an unrealistic faith. The psalm knows that we will all "walk through the valley of the shadow" . . . "the table is set in the presence of my enemies." Life is vulnerable, and faith is conflicted. Just because that is so, we need the shepherd. John Calvin said, "There is a great difference between the sleep of stupidity and the repose of faith."

"I shall not want." That is not self-confidence or false confidence. It is God-confidence.

Moreover, this psalmist was drawing on Israel's memory of what God had done for the people of God in the past. He was composing out of their tradition. Psalm 23 is woven with allusions to the memories recorded at other places in the Old Testament.

Deuteronomy 2:7 says, In all the years in the wilderness, Israel did not lack.

Exodus 15:3 says, The LORD leads Israel like a flock to His holy pasture.

Psalm 78:19 says, God prepared a table for Israel in the wilderness.

So the metaphor is not the reflection of a simple pastoral scene. It contains the theology of the sovereignty of God and the memory of God's way with the people of God.

THE FIRST-PERSON STYLE OF THE PSALM

Psalm 23 is misleading with respect to the other psalms. It is so well known and loved that it is taken to be typical and representative.

Just the opposite is true. With respect to its distinctive characteristic Psalm 23 is completely unique. No other psalm says, "My shepherd." In all the other psalms where "shepherd" is used as a metaphor for the deity, the relationship is to the community. Indeed, in all the many uses of the metaphor in the entire Old Testament, it is always "our shepherd."

What is going on in Psalm 23 is the location and recapitulation of God's relation to his people in the living of one individual person.

There is a breakthrough here that is crucial to the way that leads from the Old Testament to the New Testament and to the future of the faith. Jesus will say, "I am the good shepherd." And when he tells the parable of the Shepherd who leaves his flock to go search for the one lost sheep, it is Psalm 23 that has prepared for this drastic concentration on the individual believer.

There is also instruction here. The lesson should be that you cannot have the "my" without the "our." You must not say "my shepherd" without also and first saying "our shepherd." Sheep by nature belong to a flock, and a sheep off by itself is lost and in danger (think of the parable!). The privilege and wonders of being able to say "my shepherd" are a benefit that comes with belonging to the congregation. Psalm 100 says, "The LORD is God! It is he that made us, and we are his; we are his people, and the sheep of his pasture."

When you think about this unusual singularity of Psalm 23, it is strange that this atypical psalm should have come to be *the* psalm, loved and known best, not only in religious but in secular culture as well. It is regarded virtually as part of our cultural heritage. In my grammar school days it was a standard item of memory work along with "America the Beautiful" and the Pledge of Allegiance to the flag of the United States.

W. L. Holladay, after a lot of research, found that this general popularity of Psalm 23 is quite recent and a distinctly American phenomenon. The shepherd psalm had no particular status in the liturgy and devotions practiced during most of Christian history, until the late nineteenth century, and then primarily in America. Why? Holladay thinks the first-person-singular idiom of the psalm fitted the individualism emerging in America—the independence of the individual from any essential identity with church or state.

His facts are certainly correct. Is his explanation also true? If so, I would like to believe that the psalm has served to inform our fierce individualism with a sense of belonging to God. And if we remember always to read and use Psalm 23 as part of the entire Psalter, it will also keep us mindful of the flock to which we belong and on which we depend.

USES OF THE PSALM

In any case my associations of Psalm 23 are primarily with occasions of the congregation, times when the community of the faithful are gathered.

First of all, with funerals and graveside services. How many times we have heard on such occasions, "Yea, though I walk through the valley of the shadow of death, I will fear no evil, for Thou art with me," and found these true and comforting words.

I grew up in a congregation that used the psalm as a reading for the Lord's Supper. As we got up from the pews to come and sit around the table to be served the bread and the cup, we said together, "Thou preparest a table before me in the presence of mine enemies. My cup runneth over. . . . Surely goodness and mercy pursue me. . . ."

One Sunday in our congregation during the morning service, when we came to the Confession of Faith where usually the Apostles' Creed is said, we said instead, and together, "The LORD is my shepherd; I shall not want." We said it as our confession of faith. That is a good and appropriate use of the psalm. We might say it every morning, for instance during Lent, as our daily declaration of who we are, and to whom we belong.

Think about it.

11

"... me, a sinner"

Psalm 51

I

The confession of sin is a regular part of the service of worship. It is the way we identify and describe ourselves to God. This practice with its understanding of the human condition is rooted in the tradition of penitential prayer that developed in Israel and became especially important during and after the exile. Psalm 51 is the primary representative of the tradition in the Psalter. It has been of enormous importance in the church's practice of penitence and has informed our thinking and praying in a remarkable way. It became the introductory Scripture for the season of Lent. A reliable estimate is that Psalm 51 has been recited in part or in whole more often through the centuries than any other psalm.

Precisely this history and familiarity may routinize and neutralize its difficulties and claims and make it seem that it comes to our lips easily and naturally. The insulation of familiarity is stripped away if we lay the text out before us, and ask with intensity and concentration whether these words can become your words. What barriers stand in the way of their appropriation? What must happen if Psalm 51 is truly to be your prayer?

Here is the psalm. I am going to read it. As I do, think about it as a prayer and ask whether it could possibly be your prayer. In the privacy of your own spirit, known only to God, be honest and searching. I do not think it is easy for these words to be meaningful and authentic for us. Some things about the psalm may even offend you—be objectionable when you ponder them as a prayer. You may feel, "That's not me," or "That's not true." But I believe this is the way Scripture always begins its work on us. It is when we feel the distance between what the Scripture says and the way we think that the real dialogue begins—and the

possibility emerges of hearing some other words than the opinions and beliefs
we already have.

> To the choirmaster. A psalm of David, when Nathan the prophet came to
> him, after he had gone in to Bathsheba.
>
> Have mercy on me, O God,
>   according to your steadfast love;
> according to your abundant mercy
>   blot out my transgressions.
> Wash me thoroughly from in iniquity,
>   and cleanse me from my sin.
>
> For I know my transgressions,
>   and my sin is ever before me.
> Against you, you alone, have I sinned,
>   and done what is evil in your sight,
> so that you are justified in your sentence
>   and blameless when you pass judgment.
> Indeed, I was born guilty,
>   a sinner when my mother conceived me.
>
> You desire truth in the inward being;
>   therefore teach me wisdom in my secret heart.
> Purge me with hyssop, and I shall be clean;
>   wash me, and I shall be whiter than snow.
> Let me hear joy and gladness;
>   let the bones that you have crushed rejoice.
> Hide your face from my sins,
>   and blot out all my iniquities.
>
> Create in me a clean heart, O God,
>   and put a new and right spirit within me.
> Do not cast me away from your presence,
>   and do not take your holy spirit from me.
> Restore to me the joy of your salvation,
>   and sustain in me a willing spirit.
>
> Then I will teach transgressors your ways,
>   and sinners will return to you.
> Deliver me from bloodshed, O God,
>   O God of my salvation,
>   and my tongue will sing aloud of your deliverance.
>
> O Lord, open my lips,
>   and my mouth will declare your praise.
> For you have no delight in sacrifice;
>   if I were to give a burnt offering, you would not be pleased.
> The sacrifice acceptable to God is a broken spirit;
>   a broken and contrite heart, O God, you will not despise.

Do good to Zion in your good pleasure;
    rebuild the walls of Jerusalem,
then you will delight in right sacrifices,
    in burnt offerings and whole burnt offerings;
    then bulls will be offered on your altar.

So there is the psalm. You can easily see what the problems are in making it our meaningful and authentic prayer. The language is so intense and personal, the scope of the confession so total, the need expressed so great that it leaves a question whether you or I could ever be the one who prays here.

In its confession of sin, the psalm is radical in three ways.

First, the David who prays is gripped with a sense of sin. It is his primary problem. He accepts it. Indeed, it is always in his mind. It has been a fact and a factor all his life. He was conceived and born in sin. It is not just a matter of what he has done, but what he is. He has done something, but that doing has become part of his identity; nay more, the failure revealed a flaw in his own being.

Second, his sin is against God, only against God. What he has done, and is, is wrong in the sight of God. Sin raises a question of his relation to God, whether God will have done with him, cast him out of God's presence, withdraw the presence and power of his Holy Spirit from his life. He is under the judgment of God. He accepts some suffering or anguish in his life as God's punishment. He knows that God is in the right, that it is just that he should be punished. God alone can blot out his transgressions, wash and purify him of his sin, cleanse him of the stain he feels on his life, deal with his guilt.

Third, the one who prays in this psalm wants to be changed. He knows that simply dealing with something he has done is not enough. God must deal with what he is. He pleads for God to create him again, to create a pure heart, to give him a new steady spirit. He wants to offer a contrite and broken spirit, not a sacrifice. He knows that a sacrifice will not do. God does not want some *thing*, but himself.

II

One way to deal with this prayer is to say that it sounds so strange and ancient as to be virtually meaningless. It is not the way we think and talk at all. Well and good that it is in the Bible and used in worship services, but people who live in a modern and secular world do not understand and express themselves in such language. We have lots of ways of talking about what is wrong with the world, with others, and sometimes ourselves, but this prayer is not one of them.

Part of the difficulty lies in unfamiliar expressions that the psalmist uses. He has, to say the least, a vocabulary different from ours. He asks God to wash him and cleanse him of transgressions, as though they were bodily filth—to purge him with something called hyssop. He speaks of the bones God has broken, of the sacrifices and burnt offerings that he might offer. It is all very Old Testament, very Israel-like, a language and mentality that come from an age and a religion of a bygone era.

But that is no surprise to us. We know the prophets and psalmists and the evangelists belong to another time and place. We are accustomed to listening to them as witnesses from the past, understanding what they say in figures, asking how faith about God and God's way is present in their sometimes quite different and difficult speech.

No! The real problem lies somewhere else. The difficulty of this prayer for modern people is simply the fact that it is a confession of sin—that something called "transgression" or "iniquity" is taken to be the central and primary problem of human life. Sin is a notion that does not have much currency out there in real everyday life. Of course, we do have problems. Everybody admits that. In terms of awareness, we are probably as problem-ridden as any generation in history, but sin is not the category by which people understand and cope with problems. Not many today would say with the psalmist, "My sin is ever before me."

To be secular and worldly means to think about life in terms of the areas and enterprises of which the human world consists. We think of ourselves as physical, psychological, social, and economic beings, and we describe our activities and problems in terms of facts and experiences in these areas. One may have hypertension, or we can't make decisions, or there is racial tension, or the stock market is unpredictable. A long list of items like that would make up a typical agenda of problems. To be modern means to believe that we can solve these problems with the resources of technical and professional skills and knowledge. Some action can be taken to cope. Physicians can cure diseases. Psychological counselors can ease our mental stress. A growth economy will secure our livelihoods. Social programs will ameliorate racism. People who understand and manage life completely in these terms can be said to be secular and modern.

My point is not that it is undesirable or bad to be secular or modern. A question can be raised about whether it really works as a total approach. But one cannot imagine it would be good to ignore the functional spheres of life, and not take whatever action seems useful and helpful to meet problems. The point is, rather, that sin as a notion to describe the problematic side of life does not arise and has no use in a consciousness that is totally shaped in this way.

Karl Menninger published some years ago a book with a rather surprising title, *Whatever Became of Sin?* He observed that the word had disappeared from public discourse, had even lost currency in some church circles. Americans, he contended, at one time had an essentially moral ethos and the sense that life is basically a moral project of accountability, and responsibility was part of the cultural heritage. He was concerned that the atrophy of a sense of sin really meant a deterioration in the self-understanding of the typical American.

But sin is not basically a moral idea. It is a religious experience. It arises and is vital and meaningful only in the context of the knowledge of God. Only where people believe that their life is lived in the presence of God, is a gift of God, is summoned and measured, is responsible and accountable to the One who is the source of life—only there does sin as experience and language rise. One of Ingmar Bergman's characters said, "Without God, everything would be okay." In a sense, that's right. Get rid of God, and you've gotten rid of any ultimate criterion for what you are and do.

When the filmmaker and actor Woody Allen was criticized publicly for an affair with the young daughter of his ex-wife, he excused himself saying, "The heart wants what it wants." Ah, yes. When you yourself are the only norm of your life, then all is permitted.

"Against you—you alone have I sinned," says the psalm. If you were not there, my God, I would not be a sinner. I might be many other things, measured and classified by other norms and relations (a vindictive father, a selfish neighbor, a greedy businessman), but I would not be a sinner. Only when life is lived in all its secular-modern aspects in awareness of the infinite righteousness and love of God would it make any sense to pray as the psalmist prays.

The psalm is really a question about life, whether all of life is lived to God—to the God who shows us the way in the Commandments and the Christ.

III

Another way to assess the prayer in Psalm 51 is to think of it as somebody else's prayer. We might read it because it is there in the Bible or recite it when it is used as a responsive reading in worship. We might, in doing so, find it interesting and instructive, but it is not really our prayer. What it says does not correspond to what we have done or what we are. The shoe doesn't fit, so why try to wear it?

We could read it as David's prayer—and leave it at that. The introduction to the psalm offers that as a possibility. The title of the psalm says that David prayed the prayer after the prophet Nathan had made him realize what he had done in his affair with Bathsheba. So it is David's prayer and not ours. It makes sense as the confession of a man who had done what he did. David had acted like a biblical J. R. Ewing (remember the TV show *Dallas*?). David committed adultery with Bathsheba, and when his crime was about to be exposed, he arranged for Uriah, her husband, to be killed. If you are a king or own a lot of oil wells, you will be tempted to do all the things you can do. So the prayer belongs to one episode in David's life. It is there in the Bible to be used by others whose failures are so great and whose guilt is so damning that they need the intensity and scope of such a prayer as their confession.

A prayer for whomever—and whenever, but not for me and not now.

A friend and colleague told me recently that he has the same kind of problem with the confession of sin in the regular Sunday worship. As he reads or listens to the confession of sin printed in the order of service, he keeps saying to himself, *These aren't things I have done. What we are saying doesn't fit me.* The confession is usually not authentic or actual for him. He doesn't recognize himself in the prayer. And it is certainly true that it is difficult to write a confession of sin for other people. Either it is too specific to speak for everybody, or it will be so general that it has no relevance.

One is more likely to feel this way if sin is thought of in a legalistic or moralistic way. Sin is a category for acts—something done or thought. It is transgression of a specific commandment or a law, failure to observe a moral principle. It is the quality of a deed, not of the doer. It is dealt with by punishment or pardon that corresponds to the deed. The Shorter Catechism says, "Sin is any want of conformity unto or transgression of the Law of God" (question 14). The way in which that definition is usually understood supports the legalistic notion of sin. Adultery is sin. Murder is sin. For confession of sin to make any sense, one has to locate in one's own life some act that breaks a rule or principle. Questions will arise about the rule, what it means, whether it applies, whether there are extenuating circumstances. For this line of thinking, Psalm 51 poses quite an enigma. What could one do to need a prayer like this?

There is another notion abroad in the land that really does make the psalm irrelevant. It claims that most of what goes wrong with us is the result of what our parents did or didn't do, or the influence of the culture. If one has learned that lesson well, confession of sin is always somebody else's!

Of course, when the psalm is read carefully, it turns out that no specific sin is mentioned. It is, rather, the bare and simple reality of sin itself that seems to be the agenda. Not a "what," but "that." From the viewpoint of the psalm, the need to locate a particular transgression or immorality does not seem to be the primary issue. It does raise a question of whether this approach really grasps what the psalm is about.

<h1 style="text-align:center">IV</h1>

Another way to look at Psalm 51 is to see it as a general prayer of repentance—a prayer given to the church through Scripture that any believer might pray—

and perhaps all should pray from time to time. That is the approach to the psalm on which its use to introduce the season of Lent is based. The psalm, this view of it would say, brings to light the first and basic truth about human beings before God. It creates a situation in which humanity appears as what it is and God appears as what God is. People are sinners. Whatever else may be said about them—and there is much else to be said—before God, we are sinners. God is gracious. Whatever else can be said about God—and there is much else to be said—God is a God of grace. If the prayer does, in fact, bring to light and put in words the true circumstances of the relationship between God and people, then nothing else can ignore or qualify or cancel the facts of this basic situation. "Have mercy on me, O God, according to your steadfast love" is the primal response of faith that underlies every other response to God.

If that is the right way to understand the psalm, the reason or occasion for using it does not depend on some wrong we have done, whether trivial or heinous. It does not depend on our feeling guilty sometimes or on an apprehension that we are not as good as other people. It depends quite simply on faith's knowledge that God deals graciously with us because we need God to do so. A sinner is simply someone who needs the grace of God. That is the evangelical truth about sin. All else that is said in the Bible and theology is elaboration and explanation of that central fact brought to light by the covenant and the cross.

If this is the right way to understand the psalm, then everything that Messiah Jesus said and did becomes relevant. There is, for instance, the story he told about two men who went to the temple to pray. One said in his prayer, "Lord, I thank Thee that I am not like other men. . . ." He spoke to God, but he was looking at his fellow men and asking God to see him just as he saw himself—in comparison to them. The other man in the story said in his prayer, "Lord, be merciful to me, a sinner." He looked to God alone and asked God to see him in terms of God's grace. He was a marvelous example of what the psalm calls "the broken and contrite spirit" that is acceptable to God—the true offering, the true sacrifice. He was the one, Jesus said, who went down to his house, justified, in the right, with the only righteousness possible before God: trust in the grace of God.

Once Jesus said, "Those who are well do not need a physician; only those who are sick do. I did not come to call the righteous but sinners." He left his hearers to decide whether he meant that there were some who did not need the doctor. The irony in his remark, of course, is that the sinners who need him are the ones who may be made righteous—and those who call themselves righteous and do not need the grace of God are, in fact, the ones in the greatest need of that grace.

If this is the right way to understand the psalm, then we are dealing here with one of the most difficult and important perceptions of Christian belief—the universality and inevitability of sin in the human condition. When the psalmist says, "I was born in iniquity and in sin my mother conceived me," he does not mean that his conception was a sinful act on his mother's part, or that his sinfulness is a biological heritage. The verse means that sin was there in the human fabric from the beginning of his life, a factor of his whole existence.

All humans are sinful. Every human act is conditioned by sin. That such is the human predicament is affirmed by the experience of believers and the reflection of theologians through the centuries. Chapters 2 and 3 of Genesis talk about it in the form of symbolical story. Paul wrestles with it in the great meditation of Romans 7. And it seems to work this way.

Human beings are created finite and free. We could take our limitations as a reason to trust God. We could use our freedom to be responsible to God. We could, to use the language of Jesus, enter the kingdom of God like a little child. But a self that is finite and free seems always to use what freedom it has to try to cope with its limitations; a whole range of actions emerge, none of which is wholly the love of God.

This does not mean that there are no good people or no good in people, or that all people are on the same moral level, or that there is no point in doing good, or any of such gloomy or silly things. It does mean that it makes sense for all of us to pray as Psalm 51 does, asking God to be merciful to us sinners. And we speak our truest need when we ask, "Create in me a clean heart, O God, and put a new and right spirit within me."

12

Mercy Joined to Loving-Kindness

Psalm 103

One of the most important developments in the history of the use of *hesed* (loving-kindness or steadfast love) for the way of God in the biblical vocabulary of faith is its association with the words that mean compassion, tender mercy. In word pairs, *hesed* is usually associated with faithfulness, dependability. But through certain experiences Israel came to know that the Lord's *hesed* was joined to a merciful and tender caring upon which their very existence depended.

The most important witness to this realization is the self-proclamation of the Lord to Moses that the biblical authors have incorporated at the climax of the story about the disaster of Israel's worship of the golden calf. As the theological resolution to this incredible failure on the part of the covenant people, the Lord proclaimed the Lord! "The LORD, the LORD, a God merciful and gracious . . . abounding in steadfast love and faithfulness" (Exod. 34:6). This crucial self-proclamation by God can be regarded as a theological reflection that expounds the relation between *hesed* and *rachamim* (compassion).

Psalm 103 is the perennial psalm of the mercy of God in every age; in liturgical contexts from Sunday service to the graveside, in the prayers of the simple and sophisticated, this psalm bears forth the presence of God whose ways impel the soul to bless the Lord. The reason for the usefulness of the psalm is its subject and the way that subject is developed in a poem of subtle allusions and aesthetic power.

The larger structure is that of a hymn of praise. The psalm begins and concludes with a summons to praise (vv. 1–2 and 20–22). The opening summons ends with a call not to forget the benefits of the Lord. The body of the hymn (vv. 3–19) answers that call with a recalling, affirming review of the Lord's benefits. There are four parts in the body, distinguished by style and subject. Verses 3–5 continue the direct address to the soul and list in a series of clauses the benefits of the Lord. Verses 6–9 describe the dealings of the Lord with Israel. In verses 10–14, the "I" of the opening sentence becomes a "we" who describe the dealings of the Lord with them. In verses 15–18, there is a reflection on the contrast between the steadfast love of the Lord and the existence of mortals. Verse 19 proclaims the reign of the Lord over all, a proclamation that leads into the concluding summons, addressed to the heavenly officers of the Lord's rule (vv. 20–24).

This review of the Lord's dealings may seem somewhat random in style and subject, but it is integrated not only as a form of remembering instead of forgetting but also by a common theme. The theme is the way in which the loving-kindness (*hesed*) of the Lord has prevailed over Israel's sinfulness. The term appears as a central notion in all four parts of the body (vv. 4, 8, 11, 17), and is lifted up as the central theme in part 4. The way the Lord deals with sin opens the first and third parts (vv. 3, 10), and is the underlying concern of the whole. The psalm can be viewed as a poem written in hymnic style on the text of Exodus 34:6–7 by a member of a circle who believed that the Lord has shown in all his dealings with Israel how his loving-kindness prevails over their sin. The poem's reflective perspective on the past is evident in the references to events and texts from the book of Exodus (vv. 6–8, 17–18) and by the way it draws on the prophecy in Isaiah 40–66 (vv. 9, 11, 15).

2. "Bless the Lord" is a synonym for "praise the Lord." It means to do good to God by speaking of God's ways and works in adoration and gratitude. God's own doing is the content with which human beings bless God. The blessing of the Lord is to take the form of a recital of his "dealings," his acts in response to human conditions and actions (RSV "benefits"; the same Hebrew root appears in "requite" in v. 10). The recitation will be a way to avoid the grievous error of "forgetting." "Forgetting" and "remembering" the Lord are not primarily cognitive acts. To remember the works of the Lord is to make them imaginatively present to mind and will, so that they become the reality in terms of which one believes, feels, and decides. To forget is the opposite. The body of the hymn is an act of that kind of remembering. Those who sing it place themselves in the presence of the God evoked in its description and reckon with his *hesed* as the condition under which they, sinners, may live.

3. The list of the Lord's dealings in verses 3–5 is composed of items that are part of one process. They all stand under the rubric "forgive" in the first clause and flow from that. In sequence they outline the course of a forgiveness that heals and redeems life from threatening death, so adorning life with steadfast love and mercy and making it possible to experience life as good—with the result that life is renewed. The simile of the eagle probably refers to the bird's soaring, effortless flight, and is simply a way of characterizing the renewed life. Note the simile in Isaiah 40:31. The pattern in the sequence is that of a

recovery from disease that is experienced and interpreted as the Lord's *hesed*-working healing as the expression of forgiveness of sin. But this report on healing and restoration is not made as the report of a particular experience of an individual, but rather takes the form of a characterization of the Lord and what the Lord does for the soul. Notice the inclusive "all" in verses 2–3 and the present tense of the verbs. The prophets used the vocabulary of disease and healing to interpret the Lord's way with sinful Israel (e.g., Isa. 57:14–21; Jer. 16:4; 14:18). It is likely in light of the rest of the psalm that the individual who speaks here is personifying corporate experience.

4. The four statements about the Lord in verses 6–9 also seem to be a catena of separate items. But verses 7–8 are a clue to their unity. Verse 7 refers to the time of the exodus from Egypt, and verse 8 is a citation of Exodus 34:6–7 (see also Num. 14:18; Ps. 86:15) where in the incident of the golden calf Moses and Israel learned that their existence depended on the great loving-kindness of God in dealing with their sinfulness. The statement in verse 9 that anger is not the Lord's normal attitude draws again on Isaiah 57:14–21 (specifically v. 16) and reflects the exilic experience. Together the four statements are a reading of the exodus tradition in light of the exilic experience. The Lord sets things right for the "oppressed" (Jer. 50:33 uses the term for the exiles), and deals with their sin in mercy and grace, not retaining his anger. It is this understanding of God's self-revelation in the exodus and return from exile that is expressed in the following verse 10.

5. "Not according to our sins has he treated us, and not according to our iniquities has he dealt with us!" Verse 10 is the joyous confession that stands at the center of the psalm. The reflection on the Lord's dealings in verses 3–9 leads to it, and the rest of the psalm flows from it. The confession is put in negatives to throw into relief what could have been, and indeed should have been. The Lord would have been justified in dealing with them according to their sins. The marvelous thing for which the psalm blesses the Lord is that he did not. It is to account for this astonishing fact that the psalm speaks of the *hesed* of the Lord in conjunction with his *rahamin* (RSV "mercy" in v. 4, "merciful" in v. 8, and "pity" in v. 13) and graciousness (*hanun*, v. 8). The result is that the *hesed* of the Lord (his loyalty to those with whom he has established a relation) is understood all the more as an expression of the very character of God himself and less as any obligation in which he has involved himself.

Verse 10 is elaborated and expounded by three statements that use similes to explain the wonder of it. The greatness of the Lord's *hesed* is like the height of the heaven over earth (note the simile in Isa. 55:9). The distance the Lord has put between them and their sins is like the distance of east from west (a powerful metaphor for forgiveness, found also in the hymn that concludes the book of Micah, a hymn that has a number of similarities to Ps. 103). The Lord's compassion manifest in forgiving their sins is like the compassion a father shows children. Compassion is not primarily a feeling that arises from the physiology of a parent, a biological urge; it is rather a willed act of one who is superior to and responsible for another. Both these characteristics inform the surprising explanatory statement (v. 14) attached to verse 13 that says that the Lord has parentlike compassion because he made us of dust. The appeal is not to the election of Israel but to the creation of the human being. As Creator, the Lord is superior to and responsible for—and shows both in his compassion.

In this section (vv. 10–14), the poet begins to say "we" instead of "I"; that is, he speaks in the name of a group. The experiences, traditions, and beliefs he celebrates are not private and personal. They are his as part of the group. In this sense, the hymn is both individual and corporate. The group is named in verses 11, 13, and 17; they are "ones who fear the Lord." The term belongs to a group within the national and cultic community; it designates a stance and a conduct that calls for more in belief and piety than national identity and cultic custom involve. It is the theology of this group that is expressed in this and a number of other psalms. The way the poet speaks of his community may seem to imply that the Lord's forgiveness is based on and dependent upon their fear of the Lord. But a closer reading shows that the opposite is the case; they fear the Lord because they have recognized the triumph of God's *hesed* over them as sinners. The only basis they claim in themselves for the Lord's compassion is that they are formed of dust, an expression of humility before God that is typical of their piety. Psalm 30 may be compared at this point.

6. Verse 15 picks up the theme of the finitude of the mortal and uses it to introduce a contrast between the finitude of the human and the infinitude of the Lord's *hesed* (vv. 15–18). The human is transient, like the flower that blooms, withers, and disappears. The simile probably is an appropriation of Isaiah 40:6–7, which speaks of the transience of human *hesed*. But the Lord's *hesed*, shown in righteous acts of deliverance, is not limited by time. Just as the *hesed* of the Lord prevailed over their sin in the past, it will accompany their future down through the generations of their children. Here the poet does enter a reservation, an "if," a condition for the continuity of the Lord's loving-kindness. Citing the conclusion of the second commandment (Exod. 20:6; Deut. 7:9), he says it is to those who respond to the Lord's *hesed* by living according to the precepts of his covenants (used here in the sense of torah) that the righteous deliverance of the Lord will come. There is a dialectic in the way the *hesed* of the Lord is understood by the fearers of the Lord, a tension within it that must be recognized. It contains a compassion that deals with human frailty and forgiveness, and it contains an authority that deals with human independence in requiring that compassion and mercy bind the beneficiaries of *hesed* the more to the deity of the Lord. The poet has meditated on Exodus 34:6–7, where the

Lord proclaims the Lord as a God who both forgives the sinner and does not clear the guilty, and he alludes to the commandments that make it starkly clear that the purpose of the God of Exodus is that all who in any sense have been brought out of Egypt shall have the Lord as God, the Lord alone.

It is this turn to the authority of God that leads to the proclamation of the heavenly reign of the Lord over all (v. 19) that concludes the body of the hymn. It is the psalmic way of speaking of the exclusive and comprehensive deity of the Lord. Everything—forgiveness and covenant—is based on that rule and serves the purposes of that reign. This is what "those who fear the Lord" know at the deepest level of their faith.

The proclamation of the Lord's heavenly reign (v. 19) leads into the concluding summons to bless the Lord (vv. 20–22). Having described the way in which his community in their human lives exist under the rules of the Lord's *hesed*, the psalmist dares to call on all those heavenly servants of the Lord's word and will with whom Israel's theological imagination staff their vision of the divine royal court. He even adds the created works of the heavenly king to complete the comprehensiveness of the praise of the Lord. In doing so he recognizes that his praise as liturgist for his community is only a small part of the praise that sounds in heaven and on earth. At the end of the psalm, it is clear that to remember the dealings of the Lord always leads to the proclamation of the kingdom of God.

13

There the Blessing

An Exposition of Psalm 133

Psalm 133 may seem too slight a text for an expository interpretation to honor Patrick Dwight Miller, especially in the light of our long relationship. He has been a memorable student, a valued colleague in teaching and publication, and a cherished friend over the course of most of our lives. But there is something about this little psalm that signals a quality of our relationship that makes the choice of the psalm appropriate. Note, for instance, that one possible rendering of the second colon of verse 1 is "when brothers live in harmony." But there are also more particular reasons for the choice. An illuminating interpretative context for elements of Psalm 133 can be found in the book of Deuteronomy, thus connecting two biblical books that have been a special occupation of Miller.[1] The exposition draws on associations out of a personal history that he shares and will recognize. Finally, attention here to the use of the psalm in the continuing community of faith recognizes Miller's emphatic concern with the role of psalmody in the church.

THE INTERACTION OF TEXT AND
CONTEXT IN THE PSALMS

Years ago, Darby Fulton, who was the executive of the Board of World Missions of the then Presbyterian Church U.S., told about an experience he had in Korea just after the Second World War. He was on a long, slow trip in a crowded train; the passengers pressed together in facing benches. He spoke not a word of Korean and could not share in the conversation of his fellow travelers. To redeem the time, he got out a Bible and began to read. The passenger who faced him broke into smiles, began to say something, and also produced a

Bible. They recognized each other as brothers in the faith, but they could not exchange a meaningful word. After a long, awkward pause, the Korean opened his Bible and pointed to a passage. Darby recognized the psalms and by counting back from the end of the Korean Bible he came to the one that begins, "Behold how good and how pleasant it is for brethren to dwell together in unity!" (Ps. 133:1; AV). The psalm said for the two what they felt in the encounter and could not say to each other. Its text interpreted the occasion, and its words were reread by the occasion. Text and context together created a moment of meaning.

This little story captures one personal intimate minute in the long history of psalmody. But it illustrates the transition whose endless repetition composes the course of psalmody through the centuries. Wherever a psalm was used as the language of prayer and praise, its text proposed a reading of people and occasion, and its words were reread in light of the people and occasion. Notwithstanding its translation into many languages, the unchanging psalm and changing setting have interacted to create ever-new meanings.

This interaction of text and context holds true, of course, for the process of interpretation in general. But it is significant for psalmody in a special way because the texts of the psalms are not only interpreted as is the case with other Scripture. The psalms are also used as our language in praise and prayer. The interaction between text and context happens in the use of a psalm; it is enacted in the activities of praise and prayer. The psalm reads the reader as the reader reads the psalm.

It has long been an axiom of contemporary hermeneutical discussion that "a text has a life of its own." The force of the axiom is ambiguous, and one must deal with it carefully in the case of psalmody. It is possible to err on either side of the ambiguity. On the one hand, the axiom argues that a text has a capacity for meaning that is not bound to the intention of its author or the circumstances of its composition. The history of psalmody is a massive illustration of the truth of that argument. Any dogmatic historicism that will allow validity alone to an "original meaning" is forced to deny truthfulness to the practice of psalmody. On the other hand, the axiom has also been used to claim that a text is a blank formula to which readers and interpretation bring and create the meaning. But this is seriously to underestimate the effect and efficiency of the vocabulary, syntax, and structure of the text. The use of a psalm is not only an occasion for thought. The psalm proposes an agenda, a direction, and a stance for thought.

For instance, Psalm 118:17, says, "I shall not die, but I shall live, and recount the deeds of the LORD." The sentence is a fundamental expression of faith that the prospect of life instead of death has been created by the saving work of the

Lord. This is its agenda, direction, and stance. When that line was sung by the faithful in Israel, its words interpreted the situation created by the return from exile. The community had been given life instead of death. When that line was shouted by Christians celebrating Easter, its words interpreted the situation created by the death and resurrection of Christ. The contexts provided different construals of the words and their reference. But in both the verse provides the language that interprets the existence of those who sing it as a possibility created by the salvation of God.

TEXT AND CONTEMPORARY CONTEXT IN PSALM 133

Psalm 133 is a veritable fabric of semantic possibilities: its vocabulary and syntax are threads that can be woven into several constructions. Its literary structure is composed of an exclamation (v. 1) whose content is elaborated by two (or three) similes (vv. 2–3a) and supported by a declaration (v. 3b).

The exclamation is a value statement: "Behold, how good and pleasant it is when brothers dwell in unity" (v. 1; RSV). All the words in the subordinate clause have more than one possible sense. "Brothers" can mean children of common parents, "kin" in an extended family, or "kindred" (NRSV) in an extended sense in a larger social unit. "Dwell" can mean "sit," "remain," or "reside." "In unity" translates a Hebrew adverb that can mean simply "in proximity," but often means "in harmony."

The similes draw comparisons to evoke associations that actualize the value-adjectives "good and pleasant." The effect of "the precious oil upon the head" (v. 2a) and "the dew of Hermon . . . on the mountains of Zion" (v. 3a) is clear enough in Israel's aesthetic experience. The connotation of "the beard of Aaron, running down on the collar of his robes" (v. 2b) is puzzling in the context. Is it an appositional phrase used to identify the beard in the first simile or intended to be a second simile on its own? And how does the reference to the high priest's beard fit with the two similes that call on general experience? All three phrases employ the participle "coming/running down" (*yōrēd*), which seems to anticipate the final declaration and its "blessing" that comes down from God, thus functioning in relation to the end of the psalm as well as its beginning.

The concluding clause is a theological statement: "For there the LORD has commanded the blessing, life for evermore."[2] Contemporary translations render "commanded" as "ordained" (NRSV) or "bestows" (REB) to avoid the problem of "the blessing" as direct object of a verb usually addressed to a person. To what place does the emphatic adverb "there" (*šām*) refer? If it refers to Zion, the most proximate place in the psalm's syntax, then how does the theological statement support the opening observation—unless Zion is the place where brothers/kindred sit/dwell?

My interest in Psalm 133, and the reason for selecting it as an illustration, grows out of my own personal experience. I was nurtured and reared in a small communion that originated in one of the early splits in the Church of Scotland—the Associate Reformed Presbyterian Church. And, mind you, "Reformed" added on to Presbyterian meant that our fathers and mothers in the faith had thought that the rest of the Church of Scotland was not reformed enough. One of our doctrines was an exclusive psalmody; we sang no hymns—only the very songs of Scripture would do for the praise of the Lord. When we celebrated the Lord's Supper, we always used Psalm 133. A long table was set up across the front of the church. After the words of institution had been read, an elder would stand up, strike a tuning fork, and begin to sing the metrical version of the psalm: "Behold, how good a thing it is/And how becoming well/Together such as brethren are/In unity to dwell." The congregation would take up the verses, and to their rhythm we would assemble at the table as one family.

I can still without the slightest difficulty hear the sounds and remember the scene. In the years before I was admitted to the Lord's Supper as a communicant, and had to wait in the pew while the rest of the congregation was at the table, I used to ponder the strange language of the psalm, and wonder what it was all about—those words about Herman's dew, and precious ointment on the head, the beard of Aaron. Childlike, I dreamed up my own associations. In those years, Brilliantine and other hair oils were in, and beards were out.

I think it was in the midst of such ruminations that one of the questions with which I am concerned began to form, because the psalm did, after all, grow on one. In spite of its comic strangeness to me, I began to ask, "What gave the psalm a place in our celebration of the Lord's Supper?" There was—and is—in its chiseled brevity a poignancy and a promise, a depth and power that made of our gathering and actions something that they would not have been without its language. What is there in the language of the poem that made it appropriate in the context of our celebration—and even more, gave it the capacity to appropriate and redefine our situation in line with a past out of which it came—and a future toward which it tends? Here is a text that could easily be more than two and a half millennia old. It has a history of use that reaches through innumerable phases of cultural change. What has made it endure? What constant of the human condition is captured in its words? What need and possibility are evoked by its lines to be addressed by the reality of which faith speaks?

TEXT AND ANCIENT CONTEXT IN PSALM 133

The clue to the first stage of the psalm's history lies in a tension in the psalm itself. Within its brief movement there is an incongruity in the genre of its language. It begins with the idiom, vocabulary, and values of folk wisdom and concludes with those of the cultic community of Israel. The title given to the psalms in the collection to which Psalm 133 belongs is "song of ascents," literally "a song for the goings-up," or more freely, "a song to be sung on the pilgrim's way up to Jerusalem to celebrate one of the annual festivals." But judged by form-critical criteria the opening sentence does not fit that definition, does not belong to any of the genres of expression at home in the life of praise, prayer, and liturgy.

"How very good and pleasant it is when kindred live together in unity! It is like the precious oil on the head, running down upon the beard." In style and intention such an exclamation belongs to old folk wisdom, the didactic tradition cultivated by most people especially during the early stages of their cultural history. It was the business of old wisdom to observe the course of life, to perceive how things worked, to discern the better ways to steer living through its manifold problems and possibilities. The product of such folk wisdom was the basic proverb that expressed the wisdom of many and the wit of one, a saying like, "One reaps what one sows," and "A penny saved is a penny earned." One form in which such proverbs were cast was an observation about what is good. Many sentences of this particular kind are collected in the book of Proverbs. But they are also found in collections of sayings from both Egyptian and Babylonian origins. Like folk wisdom itself, the pattern and purpose of these sentences belong to human culture generally and are not restricted to any one ethnic or religious tradition. Old proverbs were coined and taught and repeated as the common instruments for discerning the possibilities of living and knowing the values inherent in choices of conduct.

The simile or comparison is a frequent element of proverbial style. By putting one thing that is known in experience alongside that which is to be understood, the latter is illuminated and perception is aided. Incidentally, "the best oil on the head" is a motif from the rituals of guest and host in the biblical world.[3] The guest who received the best oil for his head in such quantity that it ran down on the beard had the pleasure of knowing that his host meant to do him the highest honor. That is how good it is when brothers live together.

It is possible to know what the social reference of this saying was. The clause "when brothers live together" occurs in only one other place in classical Hebrew literature, Deuteronomy 25:5. There the clause is used in connection with the legal tradition that defines and regulates the early institution generally called levirate marriage. In that context, the phrase refers to the arrangement in a clan or kinship culture in which the sons and grandsons of a father continued to live as a social unit, occupying and tending the same inheritance.[4] The saying speaks of this kinship community and observes that, when its members dwell in unity, that is good. "Good," the favorite value term in such sayings, characterizes those things that support and enrich life instead of diminishing it. It involves no more and no less than what we speak of as "the common welfare." The members of such a community were bound to one another by a mutual ethic, a tradition of obligations that were inherent in the kinship relationship. When they lived up to and fulfilled that mutuality, life was more secure and whole.

When marauding brigands raided their territory, the entire clan would gather for common defense. Their unity meant strength for the protection of life. Or when lions ravaged the flock of Uncle Jedidah, all the kinsmen would together furnish him with a ram and flock of ewes for a fresh start. Unity meant the will to bear one another's burdens. When sorrow and death came unto some family in the clan, the entire kinship group would rally in sympathy and succor. In the presence of death, life was supported by the fellowship of concern and help. Those of us who grew up in rural settings have experienced themselves how the society of the larger family makes for a more abundant and durable life. And, of course, the larger family can also create problems.

The very fact that the saying should be transmitted as instruction about life is an explicit recognition that kindred did not always live in life-enhancing solidarity. The early Hebrews had the primal paradigm of Cain and Abel to instruct them about the other possibility. When brothers acted out of self-interest instead of community interest, that made for death. But how very good it is when the living of all is woven in a fabric of unity. For each it meant having a place of honor in the community life, like the guest who was honored with the best oil.

The recognition of the social reference of the saying uncovers, I think, the first dimension of Psalm 133 that gives it an abiding vitality and makes it resonate in other later times and circumstances. The subject of the saying is the relation between human interdependence and life, and obversely, the relation between human selfishness and death. It articulates in the simplest way a perception that is valid for every social unit in human history from the smallest to the largest and most complex: life is of value, so the very fact of life obligates. Actions diminish or increase the life of others. So you can live up to life only by a unity composed of awareness of the other and commitment to the other. This is true for the old kinship clan and true for the global village. It is something we all know—and yet still have to learn. The perception is accessible to any thoughtful wisdom today, and its claims still threaten the Cain in every one of us. The concern with life as a "good" is implicit in the first line of the psalm and waits the further statement of the last line.

TEXT AND DEUTERONOMIC
CONTEXT IN PSALM 133

The old wisdom saying and its perception are woven into a poem that has a larger and different social group in view. It is not necessary to insist that the saying had an independent existence in Israel's common stock of proverbs, though I suspect that was the case. It is enough to recognize the kind and substance of knowledge that the saying brings into the psalm at its beginning. The saying has been extended in a sequence of lines by the aesthetic device of repetition of themes and sentence patterns. The two added similes, which reinforce the first with new images of what is good, appear to be drawn from the cultic tradition of Jerusalem: Aaron, the name of the classic priest, and Zion, the name of Jerusalem as the elect city of God. The religious location of the chosen city of God where the priest presides over the institutions of the people of God is set alongside the social location of brothers dwelling together as its appositional definition. The reference "there" in the concluding declaration refers to Zion envisioned as the sphere in which brothers dwell in unity. And the term "brothers" in this larger context assumes a connotation characteristic of Deuteronomy. Especially in Deuteronomic rhetoric, "brothers" is a way of speaking of the people Israel as an extended family in which the traditional obligations of one sibling to another are regarded as binding between members of "the people of the LORD."[5]

Deuteronomy is, in fact, the best interpretive context for the entire final line, with its talk about enduring life as blessing that the Lord has commanded. Of course, in the entire Old Testament life is regarded as dependent on God and a gift of God. Some of the psalms, for example, speak of the life-bestowing Presence in Zion's sanctuary.[6] But it is in Deuteronomy that the phrase "The LORD will command the blessing . . ." is found.[7] And it is in Deuteronomic address that command and blessing and life are brought together as interdependent motifs.[8] It is characteristic of Deuteronomy that life is related to obedience to the commandments of God.[9]

These congruencies with deuteronomic theological tradition suggest the answers to a crucial question: how was this good and pleasant unity that is the manifestation and experience of enduring life to be accomplished by this larger and diverse family? The answer lay in the exhortation "See, I have set before you today life and prosperity, death and adversity. [Therefore] choose life, that you and your descendants may live, loving the LORD your God, obeying his voice, and holding fast to him; for that means life to you . . ." (Deut. 30:15–20). The torah was the Lord's provision of a center and a conduct, a basis of life and a way of living for a conflicted family of "brothers." Hear the torah, and one heard the blessing of abiding life commanded. Psalm 133 thinks of Israel not just as a nation but as a social unit with a transcendent source. The relational ethos of blood kinship is transcended. The fabric of interdependence that involves identity with the other and responsibility for the other overruns the old boundaries that define and limit living.

The psalm's content and title and the collection of "songs of ascent" in which it stands all point to the use for which it was composed. The occasion was probably the pilgrimage to the holy city to celebrate Tabernacles, the festival in which the pilgrims built booths and dwelt together during its course to enact their identity as community created by the salvation of God. It is an anthem whose proper context is that place where movement toward God's promise of the unity required for life becomes visible.

In imagination one can hear the measures of the psalm echoing across the ridges around Jerusalem at festival time—Israelites on pilgrimage because they had long since learned it was not enough to be kindred or neighbors or fellow citizens of one kingdom. The centrifugal forces always at work in their mortality tore them apart, set tribe against tribe, rich against poor, resident against stranger, strong over weak. But in the covenant place they heard the message: "Hear O Israel: the LORD is our God, the LORD alone" (Deut. 6:4) and faced the power who, against all that fragmented, drew them together. And in the covenant exhortation they were taught "the path that the LORD your God has commanded you, so that you may live . . ." (Deut. 5:33) and learned the guidelines for living together. When the covenant claimed them, life won and the history of God in their living became a little stronger.

TEXT AND ONGOING CONTEXTS IN PSALM 133

There is, as far as I can find, no specific allusion to Psalm 133 in the literature of the New Testament, as is the case with so many other of the psalms. But its theme and concern appear in many places. In a letter to one of the early Christian communities the writer observed, "We know we have passed from death to life, because we love one another" (literally: "the brethren" [tous adelphous]) (1 John 3:14). If we ask how this new religious community learned that, and how they came to be calling one another brothers and sisters, the best place to go for an answer is a story about Jesus of Nazareth (Mark 3:31–35). During the controversy and confusion provoked by his activity, his family feared he lost his mind and came to the house where he was. They stood outside and called to him. A crowd was sitting around him and they said to him, "Your mother and your brothers and sisters are outside asking for you." He replied, "Who are my mother and my brothers?" He looked around on those who sat about him and said, "Here are my mother and my brothers. Whoever does the will of God is my brother and sister and mother." This abrupt rupture of the kinship relation and its interests, and its replacement by another kinship group created by his person and the enactment of God's will in his mission, is astonishing. It signals the subordination of every natural and ethnic and national dependence for identity and ethos to a new overarching community centered solely in him. It was a move that impelled the reach of the Christian community across every boundary in the societies and nations of the Roman Empire. Now it was possible to sing, "How good and pleasant it is when brothers and sisters live in unity" within new horizons of expectation that stretched toward the whole family of humanity.

With its passage through that context, Psalm 133 entered the history of Christian praise and thought, and, of course, it lived on in the worship and piety of Judaism. It was incorporated into the cycle of lectionary readings in synagogue and church to be heard again and again in a repetition that colored the consciousness of many generations. The poem was translated, first into Greek and Latin, then into other languages, cast in the form of hymns and paraphrases. Of the countless contexts in which it was used, some are still visible. I mention several of these only as illustrations.

Augustine noted in the fifth century that "the sound of the first verse is so sweet that it is chanted by persons who know nothing of the rest of the Psalter."[10] In what was certainly a bit of an overstatement he also said that the psalm gave birth to the monasteries; it was like a trumpet call to those who wished to dwell together as brethren. So in those days Psalm 133 had become a lovely slogan to articulate the joy believers experienced in a community that had more purchase on the future than the dying Roman culture around them, and it had become one of the texts by which the emerging monastic communities understood their character and purpose.

John Calvin's passion for biblical praise gave the psalms new vitality in congregational worship. Many in the early Reformation committed metrical versions of the entire Psalter to memory. In one of the orders for the celebration of the Lord's Supper, the first verse of Psalm 133 was said, just after the words of institution, as "The Peace." Its use interpreted the sacramental communion as the constitution of a family through whose unity God bestowed the blessing of life.

In the *Book of Common Prayer*, Psalm 133 is designated as a psalm for use in the services of Christian Unity. In such a context it is a two-edged sword. It speaks judgment on the church's vulnerability to the power of race and nation and particular history to define the catholic fellowship by division. But it remains a gracious, encouraging invitation to pilgrimage toward the center that unites.

Finally, one illustration from a contemporary setting: Some years ago in Little Rock, Arkansas, the synagogue belonging to the congregation of Beth

Ahabah burned down. An arrangement was worked out for the Jewish congregation to share the building of the Second Presbyterian Church. On Saturday, the Jews worshiped in the building and called it a synagogue; on Sunday, the Presbyterians worshiped there and called it a church. The alternation lasted several years. As time passed the alternation changed to a conversation, and the conversation, to discovery of each other that had remarkable effect on both communities. When the new synagogue was dedicated, the Presbyterians were honored guests and in the service were given a banner that now hangs in their church. On it Psalm 133:1 is inscribed in Hebrew:

מה טוב ומה נעים שבת אחים גם יחד

In all these contexts, a micro-fraction of the whole history, Psalm 133 brings two contributions. First, it elicits and forms into language the original insight of the old saying with which it begins. Where that occurs, consciousness is focused on the need and the innate longing for a unity of persons equal to the demands of life. Second, it sets the predicament and possibility of human existence in the perspective of faith in the covenant-making God of Israel and the community-forming event of Jesus Christ. The psalm reveals that God is the power who withholds life from the rejection of interdependence and the source who provides life as a blessing when people let the divine purpose bring them together.

The two contributions generate an eschatological tension. In every occasion where the truth of the psalm's wisdom is acknowledged and the power of the promise is believed, a sense of pilgrimage is created, a movement toward a place where the family of humankind shall appear. Such occasions become a foretaste, an earnest, a proleptic and symbolic enactment of an environment defined alone by the human need for life and the divine will to bless.

14

"He Comes to Reign"

Psalms 82, 24, and 98

The biblical texts before us are three psalms that celebrate God's reign as king, psalms that have as their theme "the kingdom of God." That theme is, of course, one of the overarching motifs of the Bible's theological unity. Its first clear articulation is heard at the climax of the exodus when the rescued Israel stands on the further side of the Red Sea and sings a psalm that concludes, "YHWH will reign forever and ever." At Sinai, Israel becomes the people of God by a covenant that gives them a theo-political social form as the people ruled by YHWH. The prophets are messengers of that sovereignty to its constituents. Jesus by teaching and deed opens the eyes of people to their situation in the reign of God. The book of Revelation concludes the canon with the eschatological shout "The kingdoms of this world have become the kingdoms of our Lord and of his Christ."

In the midst of this canonical continuity, the psalms, both as a book and in their presence scattered through other books as well, raise hymns to the glorious king, "the LORD most high." "Sing praises to our King, sing praises, for God is the king of all the earth; sing praises with a psalm," says the Forty-seventh psalm. The reign of God is the great biblical metaphor for God's relation to the world and humanity. It is not dispensable. It can be interpreted but not eliminated. The symbol participates too much in the reality.

The metaphor and the reality it signals are essential to a spirituality that is shaped by the Bible. A candidate for nomination to the presidency once made this typical politicians' claim: "I believe the people of this country are hungry for a spiritual revival. I think they want to believe in themselves and in their government again." There seems to be a general conviction among candidates for office in America that this assessment is necessary to political success. Of course, Americans want to believe in themselves and the government of their country. The belief in tribe and self is the oldest form of paganism. It comes naturally to the human condition, whether it is thought of religiously or in a secular way.

Now, I love this land with a devotion that brings pain with it at times, and I know that what I think and feel about myself is fundamental to the way I live. But the human spirit needs a more universal and righteous setting for its consciousness than the nation if it is to be redeemed. The One Hundred-eighteenth Psalm speaks to the point: "It is better to take refuge in the LORD than to put confidence in mortals. It is better to take refuge in the LORD than to put confidence in princes." Recent experience as well as theology suggests that is good advice.

The psalms I have selected are the Eighty-second, Twenty-fourth, and Ninety-eighth. The three have in common that they speak of the kingdom of God in terms of God's coming. In this way, they show that God's reign is a recurrent happening, an eventfulness that intrudes on human life and history. The reign of God is not an institution or organization or program. It is not an abstract idea or an eternal truth. It is an unfinished drama with a past and a future, a drama composed of certain typical happenings that continue what is already begun and keep the present open on the future. The Eighty-second psalm lets us see the judgment upon the powers that dehumanize life. The Twenty-fourth shows us the way to the sanctification of life, and the Ninety-eighth offers the words of true joy that can be raised in this world as it is and in spite of what it is.

I

Psalm 82 may seem a strange choice because it is a strange text. There is not another psalm like it in the Psalter, and its subject is astonishing. It tells about the judgment and death of the gods. That subject has a resonance with the theology of the 1960s that attracted so much attention under the slogan "The Death of God." But the psalmist had taken up the general subject millennia before our time in a quite different way. He knows that the gods must die that humanity may live, and the presence of this strange psalm in the Psalter insists that word is still true.

The psalm begins by showing us a vision. God has arrived and taken his place as the head of a divine council composed of all the rest of the gods. Then in verses 2 through 7, we hear the speech of God addressed to the council, a speech composed of questions, instruction, observation, and pronouncement. Verse 8 concludes the psalm with a petition. The voices of those who behold the vision and hear the speech speak from their place on earth and cry out to God to arise and judge the earth and so enact his Lordship over all the nations.

When we look at the psalm form-critically, it is apparent that the first seven verses are the portrayal of judicial proceedings of a trial. God holds judgment in the midst of the gods; as we listen to what God says, it becomes evident that the council itself is under judgment. Everything that is said in God's address in verses 2 through 7 can be classified according to the rubrics of speech that was customary in a court. The question in verse 2, "How long will you judge unjustly and show partiality to the wicked" is the accusation. The imperatives in verses 3 and 4 do not function as instruction but rather elaborate the accusation. The imperatives itemize the norms for the right use of power. Anyone, divine or human, who exercises power over the other should do these things: give justice to the weak and the fatherless, maintain the right of the afflicted and the destitute, rescue the weak and the needy, deliver them from the hand of the wicked. Verse 5 is the verdict on the gods on trial. It is the finding of the court that the gods have neither knowledge nor understanding. They all walk about in darkness. Because of their great failure, all the foundations of the earth are shaken. Their guilt is such a threat to existence itself that their status as gods can no longer be tolerated. Finally, verse 6 is the sentence of the court, the announcement of what must be done with the guilty. The best translation of this verse would go something like, "I, myself, designated you by my word, 'Gods are you and sons of the Most High, all of you.'" The sentence says that the Lord God himself is responsible for and has authority over the other gods. They have belonged to the system of his sovereignty over all the earth, but his verdict now must be, "Nonetheless, like man you will die, like one of the high officials of an earthly government, you will fall."

Verse 8 is a petition that is found at many other places in the hymns and prayers of the Psalter, so it clearly is the language of the congregation. It stands here as the petition of the congregation at worship in response to what they have seen and heard. The trial scene and the saying of God in it have no real counterpart in the Psalter, but it is similar to many prophetic sayings that have been cast in the form of a portrayal of judicial process. It is probable that in its original use, Psalm 82 belonged at a point in the liturgy of the Temple, in which a prophet spoke verses 1 through 7 and the congregation answered liturgically verse 8. It is one clear testimony to a relation between preaching and liturgy in the Old Testament.

Admittedly, the first hurdle to understanding this psalm comes in the first verse, with its portrayal of God assuming office as judge in a divine assembly of gods. The picture simply does not belong to our thought world or our theological tradition. We are confronted instead by an imaginative drama that comes part and parcel out of the mythology and religions of the peoples of the ancient Near East, the cultural environment in which Israel lived out most of its history. The worldview of those cultures was mythopaeic and polytheistic. Their understanding of reality was always expressed in dramas that involved a plurality of gods. The problem of those cultures was not whether there be a god at all, but how all the various gods could get together to manage the affairs of the world. The notion of the divine council, a parliament of the deities, a kind of supernatural United Nations convened to debate and conclude the common affairs of the gods was one of the ways in which they dealt with this problem. We know of this divine council from the early texts from Mesopotamia and Canaan. It is a notion that is obviously widespread in the world culture, and everyone in that culture, including Israelites, would have known what scene was being portrayed. From what we are told about the procedures of this council, it was as chaotic and contradictory as its present-day counterpart that meets in New York.

In this divine assembly, the psalm says, the Lord appears and takes his place. This is difficult for us on two counts—first, because we cannot possibly with our view of reality take this divine council seriously, and, second, because with our theological tradition, we are uneasy at confronting so directly an appropriation by a believer in Old Testament times of a feature of the mythology of the ancient Near East.

However difficult the notion, the myth offers us a vision of what the psalmist would have us see. For he does not invoke the vision of the divine council simply to add Israel's god to the list of dignitaries and to enroll the Lord in the pantheon of the nations. The intention is quite the opposite. The notion of the council is being used as a vehicle for a quite different perception of reality that is a break with its culture. It is a mode of expressing a perception of God's dealing with the powers and forces of history. This portrayal of the assembly of the gods is unlike any other of which we know in ancient Near Eastern culture because it announces the permanent adjournment of the assembly and the execution of its constituency. In its own cultural world, it is an exquisitely fashioned polemic. The Lord appears at the head of the council for the purpose of passing judgment on its members. His unequivocal verdict resounds at the climax of his speech to the council: "Like men you shall die, you shall fall like any court official." The gods of the nations, the deities of every people are doomed. The history that the Lord works through his word to Israel and the church is the story of the death of the false gods. The possibility, which this psalm here gives faith, is the possibility of right faith and the answer to the question about the true identity of God.

There is more here than a simple word about monotheism, the dogmatic principle that there is only one God. The cruciality of this psalm is not shut up to an era of polytheism in which it said its word and was finished. If that were the case, it would not be in the canon. The device of the divine council is used because the process of judgment on false gods is a reality of human experience as long as the human story unfolds.

There is a profound implication behind the Lord's verdict on the gods. "You shall die like men and fall like any court official." Like men—like government functionaries. The verdict is but the naked fact: their deity is a human creation. They are the self-glorification of peoples and rules writ large on the tablet of heaven. Such gods are always with us—always because they are part of the human predicament, the ceaseless art of our feverish genius for evading the actual divine human encounter with the Father of Jesus Christ. And they are real divinities because we let them be. No matter that in our era we do not so name them because of our sophisticated modernity. It is ironic that our secular prophets who announced the death of God set up their pulpits on the edge of a swirling vortex, which spawned deities with a power that puts Baal and Marduk to shame. People have died because of them and for them by the millions. A divine pharaoh in Thebes was a piker beside an incumbent of a modern dictatorship gripped with a messianic sense of destiny. The fertility gods leer at us in the provocativeness of art and advertisement, and we all clutch to our breasts the amulets of middle-class capitalist culture because that is what really answers our truest prayers. The ancient gods have not disappeared. They have simply assumed different shapes and faces.

And yet, the Lord does not taunt our gods with their origin. In his speech, he makes only one accusation, describes but one guilt. Our gods fail with human beings. They do not make people to be true humans, nor save them when they falter. In the hands of the gods, power augments evil, while the afflicted go without compassion and the weak without help. The acid test is whether by mercy and justice they save, and the gods do not pass the test. Their failure is so colossal that the foundations of the earth are shaken.

And just here is the grace of this strange song. The Lord who dooms our gods does it in the name of his own justice and mercy. For our sakes he will not allow us any other god because our gods destroy us.

That is why the psalm is here, with all its strangeness. Faith must forever be seeing the Lord standing in the midst of the gods of the time and take up the prayer with which the psalm ends. "Rise up, O God, judge the earth; for all the nations belong to you." If you hear that ancient prayer with sensitive ears, you recognize it is not different from words more familiar—"Thy kingdom come"—and at last what do we pray for with these more familiar words than the death of our gods, that the true god may be God?

II

Psalm 24 is also unmistakably a psalm celebrating the kingship of God. In verses 7 through 9 there is a surging sequence of commands, questions, and answers that reach their climax in "Who is this King of glory? The LORD of hosts, he is the King of glory!" Ancient doors are addressed and bid make themselves open, wide and high, for this king of glory who has come to claim his right to enter through them.

All this happens at the end of the psalm, but in verses 1 through 6 other themes are heard and other transactions occur. In them, the theme of kingship is not so transparent, and the question of the right understanding of the psalm becomes a question of its unity. How does that part of it which leads up to the magnificent exchange at the end belong to its subject?

The psalm lies before us in three quite distinct parts.

Verses 1 and 2 are in genre a hymn. Their lines assert quite briefly and poetically what the nature of reality is in which all people live out their life. The earth is creation. Its existence and stability are the powerful work of the Lord, so everyone who lives in the world is utterly dependent on him. To stand on the earth, to breathe its air, to be nourished by its produce, is to live and move and have being within a sphere that is the expression of his power. That is said here at the very beginning quite independently, and yet one suspects that in some way it is prolegomena to all the rest.

In verse 3 a new section of a quite separate genre or type begins. It is composed of a question in verse 3 and an answer in verses 4 through 6.

The question is asked about the identity of those who make pilgrimage to the temple and stand as a company within that holy place. It is a question about who may, and who does, stand there. It is a question about those who recognize that all space belongs to the Lord by going to that particular space which, in the condescension of his grace, he has made the place of his presence.

The answer in verse 4 compresses into two poetic lines a description of that identity. The verse is one case of several attempts in the Old Testament to comprehend the Lord's requirements in the shortest compass. "Clean hands" designates the sphere of action, and "pure heart," the sphere of will and intent. "Not lifting up the soul to what is false" means not to have made a mistake about the identity and reality of God, not to have devoted one's existence to any kind of idolatry. "Not to have sworn deceitfully" means not to have betrayed any fellow human, but to have lived up faithfully to the obligations of all relationships. So the answer is paradigmatic. It means to be pure in action and thought, and not to have betrayed God or humanity.

And note the implication of verse 6. "Such is the generation of those who seek him, who seek the face of the God of Jacob." That verse means that living according to the formula is, in fact, seeking God. The visit to the sanctuary is not something separate and different, but the culmination of a life that has already been found by God and responds by coming to the holy place.

This liturgy, like Psalm 15, is one that would have been said over and over again at the gates of the sanctuary in an exchange between worshipers and priests, and we are not to think of it so much as a testing and qualifying, a kind of liturgical legalism to sort out who could go in and who could go out but rather a liturgy that interprets and instructs. It is carried out at the gates of the temple to proclaim that worship is the expression and culmination of life.

In verses 7 through 10 we come on yet another genre. Here is a liturgy for bringing the ark into the temple. Those who bear the ark address the gates and ask them to lift up their heads that the king of glory may come in. The choir at the gates answers back, "Who is this king of glory?" and then the procession that bears the ark responds with a proclamation, "The LORD, strong and mighty, the LORD, mighty in battle . . . the LORD of hosts, he is the King of glory!" All this language greets YHWH as the God of the ark, which symbolized his presence with the hosts of Israel in the times of their history when their existence was threatened. The Lord comes to the temple as the victor, as the one who has fought the battles of deliverance, as *Kurios Victor*, as the one who has overcome the world for the sake of salvation.

As we go through the psalm, each one of these three units, distinct as they are in genre and function, seems to stand on its own. How is it that they have come together in this psalm? Many are convinced that they were originally part of a continued ritual that was performed at the fall festival in celebration of YHWH's kingship, a ritual we can no longer reconstruct. We cannot discern the coherence of the three because the ritual context is lost.

There is, however, a theological unity. Each one of the parts of the psalm expresses a basic assumption that is integral to the entire Bible and, so, to Christianity. First is that God has created the world and, therefore, is its Lord. The second is that we have to appear before God to be questioned, how it stands with our righteousness. The third is that God comes to his own and seeks entrance. Together they are three elementary dimensions of the experience of God: that we live through God, live before God, and live with God.

But to describe the parts in this way is still too propositional, and we are left with the question "What is the dramatic unity of the theology itself?" Perhaps it will become more apparent if the psalm is read in the context of a festival whose movements and rubrics we do know. The old church used Psalm 24 to celebrate the festival of Ascension. But the newer lectionaries place it in Advent. Thinking about it in a christological and ecclesiological context in relationship to Advent helps regain the unity and discern its revelation. In that context, it functions anew as the revelation of the kingdom of God.

"The LORD owns the earth." We must say this because seeing that which beholds only this world and its possibilities is no adequate vision for Advent. The kingdom is always an expression of transcendence. The one who is beyond our world is the final truth and meaning of all that is in it, and the manger on earth is enveloped in the environment of heaven. We cannot see the Christ in the child unless the curtains are drawn back on the stable scene to disclose the whole cosmic stage on which it stands. "The earth is the LORD's."

The drama of the kingdom also has its immanent side. The psalm points not only from out of earth toward heaven, but simultaneously from out of heaven toward earth. It reaches its climax in this reverberating liturgy of command, question, and answer at the conclusion, all in preparation for the appearance of God on earth as the glorious king. When Israel sang this liturgy at the gates of the temple, they were interpreting in dramatic form the meaning of their history for faith. They were declaring in the act of worship that the God who fought its battles and saved them, the God who had joined himself to them and shared their world, is at work in history to set up his rule. The church takes this psalm for use in its Advent celebration because it knows that the Child is the Christ. There in the manger, hemmed in by all the limitations of our own life, enmeshed in the complications of our own history is God come as King. This is the immanent, historical side of the kingdom. The psalm gives us vision to know the identity of the Child as the Creator whom earth cannot contain come in human flesh to be our king.

But the revelation of the kingdom has yet one more dimension: the link between the hymn of transcendence and the liturgy of immanence are a question and an answer. The question is for us, for all who go to celebrate Advent and hope in our worship to see the Christ. "Who goes, who truly enters into the time that is fulfilled to encounter the One who fulfills it?" The distance from where we are to the manger is not geographic; it is personal. Here the final and real issue of the Advent psalm is put: where the Lord of all creation appears in time and space, the question is raised about those who go to meet him. Just as surely as the secret of the kingdom discloses the identity of the child, it also defines the identity of those who seek him.

This is the kind of person who goes to meet the King. Their hands are innocent, and their hearts are pure. They have not devoted their life to the vanity of false gods, nor have they betrayed their neighbor. They are the ideal person of the covenant. They know their Lord, they know their neighbor, and their knowledge defines their life. He only goes to greet the King whose life is a search to be ruled.

Let not our voices falter when they reach these middle measures. We are likely to quaver, go weak, and lose the harmony. But we must not. We must sing the psalm through just as it is. It is true that we are not this ideal person of the covenant. But our danger is that we fall into a stock response, a routine of despair and mortification that is the end of all pilgrimage, the blight of all obedience. "I cannot be like this, so I am hopeless. God must accept me as I am, and then I still will not be like this. All my life will be lassitude and acceptance and resignation. God may rule, the King may come, but I will not be ruled."

That faltering is a kind of blasphemy against the power of God and rebellion against his Christ. It is to refuse the drama of the kingdom and the place of our life within it. The King comes to rule us. The grace of the psalm is its very description of the ideal person of the covenant. The words are about us, for they show us why we go to seek the king at all and disclose the hunger in our hearts to find the Christ so that we may be ruled. They show us what happens to us in our going and what we become because we rise up to greet the King. "Blessed are they that hunger and thirst for righteousness for they shall be filled." "Blessed are the pure of heart for they shall see God." "They receive blessing from the Lord and righteousness from the God of their salvation."

III

Early in the history of Christian worship, Psalm 98 was chosen as the psalm for the service on Christmas day. Even in Christmas services that do not use a psalm it is almost always sung, often unrecognized as such. Isaac Watts's carol "Joy to the World" is a Christian version of Psalm 98.

In the form in which it is composed, Psalm 98 is a typical "hymn of praise," one of the literary genres of which the Psalter is composed. Most of these hymns were written following a simple literary formula or pattern: imperative verbs that summon to praise, followed by declarative sentences that state the content or reason for praise. Psalm 98 is arranged on that pattern. An opening call to sing a new song to the Lord is supported by the declaration that God has done marvelous things (v. 1). Verses 2–3 say what the marvelous deeds are and claim that at the ends of the earth people have seen them. Then, because all the earth are witnesses, the whole world—indeed, the whole creation—is summoned to join in the praise (vv. 4–8) because these marvelous deeds are the enactment of the coming of the Lord as king to rule the world in righteousness and equity (v. 9).

The thesis of the hymn is this: the marvelous deeds that the Lord has done are a revelation to all the world of the coming reign of the Lord over the earth and its peoples. Just why all should rejoice at these marvelous deeds is somewhat hidden in the contemporary way the lines that describe them are translated. Verses 2 and 3 could be translated, as some older and current versions do, rendering "salvation" instead of "victory" and "righteousness" instead of "vindication." The marvelous deeds were the saving works of the Lord's steadfast love and faithfulness to Israel. The psalmist is recalling all the times and ways from Abraham down through the return from exile that the Lord had saved Israel from the power of others and its own failures. These occasions of salvation were a revelation of the Lord's righteousness and disclosures of rule by the power behind all creation and history. Because that power is revealed as saving righteousness, the world can look forward to and hope for righteousness and justice.

The praise in Psalm 98 is "a new song." Perhaps in its historical context in Israel's late history it was called "new" because the marvelous deeds included not only the "old" saving deeds of the Exodus story, but also the new ones of Israel's return from exile to enter the promised land in a new exodus (see Isa. 40–55 on this). These events that Israel knew as deeds of the Lord were "marvelous" because in their happening human expectations were transcended and new possibilities were opened up. They not only "saved from" but they renewed the existence of the saved. A new song was called for that celebrated the new situation created by these marvelous deeds.

Note that the new song is sung in the very presence of the Lord (vv. 6, 9). The Lord is present in and through the saving deeds. They reveal God's coming as king to rule. Because God is made known in the story of saving deeds and because that story is a theme of public history, all the earth can rejoice. The power that guides the nations toward history's ultimate goal tends toward and intends righteousness and justice that make all things new. That is indeed a revelation that is a cause for joy—exuberant, inspired, renewing joy.

The New Testament witnesses saw in Jesus a continuation and climax of these salvific comings. In him, they say, God's rule has come and is present. His nativity is described in royal terms by Matthew and Luke. The loving, faithful rule of God was his constant theme. His teaching and saving work manifested its power for righteousness and justice. The gospel of Jesus Christ made known God's saving righteousness to the nations.

Because of all the correlations between psalm and witness to Jesus, Christians chose Psalm 98 as the song of praise for Christmas day. The psalm invokes a joy and provides a language and establishes a continuity in a story and sets the nativity in a universal context, all in a way that provides the profoundest disclosure of what happens in the coming of Jesus.

The genius of "Joy to the World" as a paraphrase of Psalm 98 is its power to bring to light the features of the psalm that make it so telling as the Christmas psalm. Indeed, the carol illumines the way in which the psalm interprets Christmas and Christmas interprets the psalm. The psalm says that Christmas celebrates the revelation of God's righteous salvation to all the world. Christmas testifies that the saving righteousness of God has come in the historical event of the Nativity. The coming of the reigning of God about which the psalm speaks has reached its central climax in the coming of Jesus of Nazareth.

So Psalm 98 joins Psalms 82 and 24 as liturgy for the coming reign of the Lord. Its manner and mood of joy is the complement that completes the other two.

Yes, the Lord's royal power is present and at work in those events of history and heart by which the false gods of this world are dethroned. Yes, the ruling of the Lord is at work when by the coming of his presence to us our lives are conformed to his will. But first and most of all, God reigns as Saviour. That is why his rule is reason for the seasons of joy among God's people. When jubilation breaks out and the sound of rejoicing is heard in the world—heard in spite of all the sorrow and sin and death in the world—that is both sign and manifestation of the coming kingdom of the Lord. "Joy to the World, the Saviour reigns!"

Preaching the Psalms

15

Delight in the Law

Psalm 1

Who is the man in the psalm? Who is this fellow who draws about him the skirts of his own righteousness, carefully avoids the contamination of sinners, and spends all his time gloating in the law? From the moment we hear of him we do not like him, and we indulge in a bit of our own righteous self-congratulation that we are not such a person.

But who is he? Doubtless, he is some proud Pharisee, confident by his own works that he is different from other men and secure even before God. He is a legalist, viewing life in terms of law keeping and religion as rule of what not to do. He is a lover of the dead letter, changed to the cold objectivity of what is written, untouched by the freedom of the Spirit—perhaps a fanatic scribe so fascinated with a book that he is oblivious of real life. A biblicist, a hypocrite blinded to his identity with the very sinners he despises. So he has been described by successive interpreters of the First Psalm.

Therefore we do not like him. He illustrates a narrow Judaism from which we are happily delivered, a gloomy law-religion from which we are gratefully free. Everything about him repels us; the modern in us and the Christian in us ally in rejecting him. We are free from the law and live by grace alone; the strenuous effort to keep rules and conform to patterns is not for us. We know that the letter kills, but the spirit gives life; we will not drive ourselves to the onerous chore of pondering some ancient manuscript. We have discovered that life is complex, that every ethical choice is ambivalent, that all morality is relative—so we are suspicious of his neat categories of righteousness and wickedness. We are not legalists. We are not puritans. We are not biblicists. What have we to do with this man?

The answer is, of course, "Nothing." We have nothing to do with such legalism. But this answer does not absolve us from the psalm at all. For the man whose way of life the psalm celebrates has his own question for us. Do we really know him? Or do we misunderstand him so we can reject him? Are we not blinded from the start by the suspicion that we are meant to be the man in the psalm, and fear to have it so? Are we not uneasy in the presence of his joy in God's revealed will, and threatened by his single-minded attention to it? Are we not apprehensive about where we stand when his radical line of separation between righteousness and wickedness is drawn? Are we not secretly defensive about the moral uncertainty and confusion of our own living and prefer to believe that a more effective way is impossible? How are we to understand this psalm—by passing judgment on him or having him pass judgment on us? Whose identity is the true problem? The sharp sword of this psalm's word is two-edged! What begins as a question about him ends up as a question about us.

We are meant to be the happy person in the psalm. Yes, "us!" Yes, in all seriousness, "happy." The First Psalm is no exhortation to proud legalism. It is a picture of obedience, of life according to God's way, of covenant faith, of discipleship, of submission to the yoke of God's reign. Its gracious gospel to us is that such life is possible, can be lived, precisely because God is revealed by saving us and giving us his will. This is its great presupposition without which it makes no sense at all. God's way is known, both as his way of grace with us and his way of obedience for us. It is too much our error that we want always to begin over and over again with God's forgiveness and saving work, because we are fascinated with our sin. We will not acknowledge that God has really forgiven us and justified us. We cannot afford to believe that God has done that, for then there would have to be something else. We must have justification without sanctification, gospel without law, a king without authority, Exodus 19 without 20, Paul's epistles without their end, a Passion story without a transfigured life, a call without an answer. But happy is the one whose delight is in the law of the Lord, who meditates constantly upon his law.

What is the law? In this psalm it is torah, not mere rules and legal codes. It is the instruction of God, God's instruction about God in that God creates, elects, saves, and makes covenant with us; and it is God's revealed will in making known to God's people in every time the meaning of God's good pleasure. Who is the Lord? In the Old Testament, the Lord is the God of Abraham, Isaac, Jacob, and Moses, whose righteousness is the help of Israel. In the New Testament, it is Jesus, his son, who saves the covenant people from their sin. The two are one—so the Scriptures are one—and this psalm is for us. Who then among us is not exhorted by the psalm? Who can but feel this happiness, know this delight, give themselves in single-mindedness to living meditation upon what is made known to them?

The Talmud tells a story about the strange conduct of an old rabbi. During the oral study of the Torah, when he came to the phrase "And God said," he would without exception fall into an ecstatic trance. He was so overwhelmed by the mystery and miracle that God should speak that his ecstasy hindered the school's progress. We are hardly endangered by such devout fanaticism. It may be that the idea of the "will of God" once so strong and definitive in our tradition is increasingly unreal to us. This psalm tells us that the "instruction" of God is the spring to nourish the life of the believer. The Christ who said, "If anyone thirst, let him come to me and drink," also said, "It is the Scriptures that bear witness to me."

16

On Needing the Wrath of God

Psalm 9:19

That is a very interesting prayer. Quite unusual—a man praying that man should be overcome. Of course, in reading the psalms, it becomes apparent that it is other persons whom the petitioner has in mind, not himself. Yet, because the psalmist seeks the victory of God and means—however fallibly— to put himself under God's rule, the prayer has a basic integrity. "Do not let mortals prevail!" It is a cry for the judgment of the Lord upon humanity and its ways, a petition for the wrath of God. "Put them in fear, O LORD! Let the nations know that they are [only mortal]."

The contention of the prayer is that we need the wrath of God. That seems a strange theology. How difficult for us to think it true. Anger seems so unlovely in another, an emotion to be restrained in ourselves. It is character- istic of our age that a great deal of theological talent has been uselessly devoted to explaining away the wrath of God. How foolish! We need God's wrath and can in no wise do without it. God's wrath is not human anger. God's wrath is the motive and personal reality of which judgment is the act. God's wrath is God's effective refusal to give way to human sin, to turn the world over to us.

Would we really want God to be without divine wrath and to turn the world over to us? Suppose God's wrath were not there—that we could be and do what we want, unhindered. Who here would trust themselves even to know what they wanted, if they could do whatever they pleased? "Power corrupts, and absolute power corrupts absolutely." In our day, by the unbelievable advance of scientific technology, the human will is equipped with incredible tools for self-expression. We are promised that soon human beings can control the thinking of others, plan by genetics the character of the human race in coming generations, even create life—produce a fetus in a laboratory. And of course—destroy all life.

If the human will were alone in the world? It turns out that to say "O God, let not man prevail" has a fascinating quality of trust in its very desperation. In fact, the prayer is simply one way of saying, "Thy Kingdom come; thy will be done on earth. . . ." And it helps us to understand the better what we ask for with such a petition.

A professor of modern history at Cambridge, Herbert Butterfield, wrote not too long ago: "It is essential not to have faith in human nature. Such faith is a recent heresy and a very disastrous one." He means to speak as a historian, but I suspect he proves a better theologian than theology's practitioners who are calling these days for a return to a new humanism.

At times when I sit with the congregation at worship on the Lord's day, I feel that all of us sense the dark, primeval abyss yawning before us and know in our secret hearts the horror of the way in which the human race has set its feet—sense and know without bringing it to words. What we require is the help of the psalms to give honest voice to our need: "O leave us not alone in the world. Save us from ourselves. Judge us." Then we might understand how Jesus Christ is the answer to our desperation.

17

The Agony and the Ecstasy

Psalm 13

The Thirteenth Psalm is one of the most compelling of all the psalms. It has only seven lines; it is spare and chaste in its style, the gaunt structure of its form visible at the first reading. And yet with all its terse phrases and taut movement, it does not lose, but gains, in passion and reality. The psalm is a prayer, a lament, an impatient complaint flung upward by one who can bear his agony no longer—and protests, yes, protests, that without the help of God he cannot live. But the psalm is not exhausted in lament. Indeed, the whole is made up of seething complaint and serene confession, hung together by an appeal for life to take the place of dying.

The man who prays this prayer is a Job-like figure who talks to God while lamenting that God has deserted him. His living is unbearably empty of the divine. Pain of soul and sorrow of heart are his constant companions. About him in his world there is hostility. He looks down the narrow corridor of his future and can see its lines converging on only one possibility: death. So he appeals—prays the elemental prayer—beseeches God for life in the midst of his dying. And then in ecstatic confidence he speaks of his trust, invokes his heart to rejoicing, and praises God who has dealt with him in grace.

It is just this incredible transition from anxiety to trust, from fear to faith, from pain to praise, that makes up the reality and the riddle of the psalm. Who is this one who accuses and adores God in the same breath? How is it possible to combine such contradictions in one soul?

The psalm is the answer to its own riddle. It is its own answer, if we will accept the psalm as the gift of God and read it as words given us by God. It will yield its secret on no other terms. As long as we keep it outside us, before us, as a problem; as long as we ask only historical questions (did David write it, or can I find someone or invent someone who had this experience?), it keeps

its mystery and remains an enigma. For the psalm is not written about someone who once prayed; it is itself a prayer. When we read it, the words become
our words; we are the "I" who speaks to God. Dietrich Bonhoeffer says of
this psalm and others like it that they are the answer that our Lord provides
for his disciples when they implore him, "Lord, teach us to pray." The psalm
ceases to be a problem only when it becomes a possibility for us—a way to
prayer *for us*.

Then it shows us who we are when we pray. Because we assume the prayer,
we are taught our true identity as mortals who stand on the earth and speak to
a God who is ours but never owned. Agony and adoration hung together by a
cry for life—this is the truth about us as people of faith. As the elect of God,
we are not one but two, a duality fused and merged by the knowledge that our
life depends on God. The contradiction is the enigma of the prayer because it
is the reality of faith as existence. The blessedness of this disclosure is that it
strips us of all our illusions that faith is a cure, an escape from our trouble, a
panacea for the awful anxiety and fear that belong to humanity. We would like
to think that we begin at one end of this prayer and come out the other end,
leave doubt and fear behind, and emerge in perfect trust and security. This
error is the spiritual folly that plagues our present with the pathetic hope that
tomorrow will be different. Surely faith works. Surely one day we can say, "I
believe," without having to cry out, "Lord, help my unbelief!" This is what the
world has always thought about religion, these days aided all too often by the
pious tutelage of the clergy.

In the recent past an influential New York minister spoke to a large paying
audience at our civic auditorium. The press reported the gist of his address
along these lines: The minister suggested that each of his listeners "have a fine
old time flushing out all your defeat thoughts" each day. Without defeatism,
happiness can be achieved, he said. "When you're happy, you do things right.
When you're happy, the error element is reduced. When you're happy, you're
on the ball." He recommended a program to be followed by the approximately
two thousand persons attending the forum. By following the program, he said,
listeners might well experience the finest day in their lives. He suggested to
the men that they refrain from being grumpy to their wives upon waking.
Instead, he said, throw back the covers, leap out of bed gaily, turn to your wife
and say, "Honey, I feel wonderful!" Now, she'll probably have a heart attack
and die on the spot, but she'll die happy. Then said the minister, bathe and
concentrate on getting the dirt off of body and the bad thoughts out of mind.
After describing a sprightly breakfast scene, he suggested that the wives be
picked up and swung cheerily around as the husbands departed. To which we
can only add the remark of a comic strip character on another page of the same
newspaper, "Good grief." Does faith really work like that?

Nothing in the careers of the prophets, of the letters of the apostles—or even the life of our Lord—suggests that it does. In this world as it is and in this humanity as it is, faith is more likely to bring you the tears of a Jeremiah, the stigmata of a Paul, a night in Gethsemane. The psalm is not given us to use on the rare occasions when some trouble seems to make it appropriate. It is forever appropriate for us as long as this life shall last. We do not begin at one end and come out the other. The agony and the ecstasy belong together as the secret of our identity. We are simultaneously the anxious, fearful, dying, historical people who cannot find God where we want God to be—and the elect with a second history, a salvation history, a life hid with Christ in God. "How long, O LORD," we lament into empty spaces. We also say, "Thou hast dealt graciously with me." And all the while we pray for life in our dying, pray because through the gospel we bear already in us a foretaste of the life to come. "For while we live we are always being given up to death for Jesus' sake, so that the life of Jesus may be manifested in our mortal flesh" (2 Cor. 4:11).

18

Getting a New Heart

Psalm 51

Create in me a clean heart, O God, and put a new and right spirit within me.

Psalm 51:10

This is the generation, the era, in which you can literally get a new heart. What was never possible before in human history is now possible. A person's old failing heart can be replaced with a different, better one. A competent surgeon, using knowledge and skills, the materials and techniques of scientific medicine, can do it now in two possible ways. One can have a transplant from a donor. Or eventually, if the project at the Humana Hospital Corporation is successful, one might have a mechanical heart of plastic and metal driven by an electric pump.

Whether the costs and results of replacing a human heart make the operation generally useful and desirable is still uncertain, but being alive is so precious that few questions are raised. A woman who is suffering with continuing problems of biological rejection of her transplant said recently, "Every day I live makes all the cost of every kind worthwhile."

Those of you who follow *Doonesbury* know that down in Haiti at the Baby Doc Medical College, the heart of a liberal was transplanted into the body of a conservative. The result was a patient who could not decide who he is or what he thinks about issues—and his poor wife exclaimed, "My God, he's turned into a Democrat!" But that's only the fun and games of a comic strip. In real life, the person of a patient is not expected to be affected.

We are in the third week of Lent, the season when believers pray for a new heart. Of course, for us the possibility is not an innovation. The prayer and the notion it expresses go back to the prophets and psalmists of the sixth century

171

before Christ. Taught and led by this quintessential penitential psalm, the church has prayed—and still prays—"Create a heart for me, one different from the one I have, a heart free of all that alienates me from you." But the *what* and the *why* and the *how* of the procedure sought by this prayer are so different.

What we pray for is psychic, not physical. In this prayer, and often in biblical vocabulary, "heart" does not refer merely to a part of one's body, an organ. It is that part of a person through which the self or ego comes to expression. It is thought of as the center of consciousness through which a wide range of critical, intellectual, and volitional activity comes to play. Heart is not identical with the first-person pronoun, but it is its metaphorical organ. "Heart" is the capacity through which sensibility, consciousness, and will function.

That is why I said what we pray for is psychic, instead of using the term "spiritual." "Spiritual" is a word used in so many loose meanings, often thought of as "religious," in a narrow sense, something added on to what a person is. But when you petition God to use God's creative power to produce an inalienable heart for you, you are seeking a change that goes to the very center of the self. Here the person of the penitent is expected to be affected.

Why we need a new heart is a matter of theology, not physiology. In the medical world of discourse we would say that the heart we were born with is the best we can have—and keeping it is a major concern. And when a physical heart starts to go bad, it lets the subject know with unmistakable and usually painful symptoms.

But in the biblical and liturgical world of discourse, heart problems are quite different. We are born and we grow up with, metaphorically speaking, "bad hearts"—that is, a self that, left on its own, is anxious and alienated. And because that is true, the self can never alone give the unmistakable symptoms of trouble.

The diagnosis comes from the outside. It is when the unclean sees the holy, when the inconstant sees faithfulness, when the anxious senses grace—then the trouble is first clearly known. Because we are called into covenant and hear the Commandments, because we are encountered by the Christ and hear, "follow me," for such reasons we know our need to pray, "Create a heart for me, different from the one I have." The prayer is not a venture in narcissistic penitential introspection, nor is repentance wallowing in indulgent confessions of failure. Rather they are the pilgrimage and the yearning that engage us when the vision of the kingdom of God looms before us as possibility and promise.

How we get a new heart is by divine help, not human wisdom. If your physical heart goes bad, the learning and judgment of a medical doctor is your best hope. But the pure heart, the steadfast spirit, the transformed consciousness—such come by the creative work of God. You will remember that "create" in the biblical vocabulary means "bring something into existence that was not there before." God alone is subject of the verb. Authentic creation can come from God alone.

That means we don't know how we get a new heart in the same way we can know how things work in the spheres of physics and chemistry and biology. Even the New Testament cannot settle on one way to describe this transforming work of God in the human consciousness. The apostles speak of "being a new creation in Christ Jesus," or a "second birthing," of "passing from death to life," of "putting on a new nature"—and mean the same many-faceted thing. We do know it happens. Scripture, history, and experience are witnesses. But it happens in fashions and modes as various as human personality and culture. To a mentality accustomed to asking for orderly, controllable data, it remains mysterious and intangible.

But of one thing we are certain: it happens in engagement with the risen Christ through the Holy Spirit. To pray the prayer for a new heart necessarily involves the use of the means of grace—Scripture, prayer, sacraments—as the way to let the Lord work on and shape our mentality, our consciousness. "Have this mind in you, which you have in Christ Jesus . . . ," says the apostle. To which we can only respond, "Create in me a clean heart, O God, and put a new and right spirit within me."

19

Joy to the World

Psalm 98

This psalm that we have read together is one which the church from earliest times has used during the celebration of Advent. With good reason! The Ninety-eighth Psalm is a summons to hilarious, authentic joy in the presence of the Lord who comes as King. Its words call the community of faith to raise a new song to the Lord. Sing because the Lord has wrought marvelous deeds of righteousness to save us, and that salvation is a revelation to all the earth of the secret of the kingdom. Therefore the universe is bid to join the exuberant celebration of the covenant people. Sing, make melody, shout, rejoice—before the king, for he has come to judge the earth.

The words of this psalm are a gift to us at Advent time. Here we are shown how real joy comes about. Nay more, we are drawn into that authentic joy and given the vision with which to see in his true identity him who is the one reason for any call to rejoice in such a world as the one in which we live.

The church has desperate need of that gift. We are the folk of faith who are supposed to be offering this festival and its cheering grace to the world. Our vision of its true meaning and our response to what actually has happened at Advent ought to be an open invitation to all about us to join and rejoice. But alas, it is seldom so. We have let the time degenerate into a celebration of the birthday of the baby Jesus. Its center is a créche with a doll in a manger—a pretty pathetic imitation child who has no identity or significance. The world has been beforehand with Christmas, and the truth is that we enter into the culture's festival looking about us anxiously to be reassured about our presence at this party.

But even the world knows that something is wrong. Like Simon Magus who would buy the gospel of the apostles to get its power, it has bought our Christmas in hope of acquiring its joy, and found only glitter and tinsel on its hands. According to a journalist writing in the local paper, a team of psychiatric social workers now have identified and described a new malady, "the Christmas crack-up." Its symptoms include a "reactive depression, crying jags, compulsive eating, loss of judgment." The affliction is provoked by the strains and stresses of trying to live up to Christmas. "The pressures of the modern Christmas celebration," the writer said, "largely preempted by merchants and twentieth-century journalism, is the route of the snake pit for many hapless persons." "Joy to the world!" What household here represented has not heard complaint about the inconvenient fact that this year Christmas comes on Sunday.

Yes, we need this psalm and its gift. For with its words we take up a liturgy that lifts up our eyes to behold the mighty acts of God who comes into time and space for our sakes. Divine love and power have invaded our world. The mystery of righteousness has struck from above into the below. Tyrants have been overthrown. Slaves set free. They who were no people have become the people of God, and at the climax of the invasion of the divine is the child in the manger. He is king—king in a way that preempts every other power and purpose. His appearance is the fact of God's reign. Joy is response to him, not something we do. It is not, as this year's popular Christmas ditty would have it, a feeling in our hearts. It is entry into the rule of God present in Jesus Christ. Now suffering is transformed into the power of God, sin is atoned, death is conquered. All because he appeareth. Sing unto the Lord for he has done marvelous things! He has come—to judge the earth!

Strange that the psalm should say "judge." The word sounds like a discord, a failure of melody at the end of the song. What has joy to do with judgment? The word invokes the feeling of something harsh, punitive, accusing. Can we rejoice in the presence of a king who comes to judge? Let us take care lest we impose on the word meanings from within our unredeemed world. Who is the judge? He is Jesus the Christ who gives himself for us. What is judgment? It is the kingly work of God by which God establishes God's rule. The word is part of the gift of the psalm. It is there for the sake of the world, the real world in which we must sing the psalm. The joy here thrust upon us is not other-worldly, spiritual, and therefore irrelevant. It makes us see the manger as set in the darkness of this world for the sake of the darkness of this world. It will not let us stand enraptured with nostalgia and sentiment about what happened two thousand years ago. It points us to the future to what is yet to be and even now happening. Jesus Christ has come to judge the world—*this* world—in righteousness.

That too is cause for joy. Indeed, we cannot do without this word if we are to have the gift the psalm would give us. For this present age is a massive persuasion against exultation. To rejoice within this world would be a miracle.

The opening stanza of Christina Rossetti's nativity poem is, for me, the most compelling description of the setting of Advent.

In the bleak mid-winter, frosty wind made moan
Earth stood hard as iron, water like a stone
Snow had fallen, snow on snow, snow on snow
In the bleak mid-winter, long ago!

Long ago—and now! Winter is still upon the world. Earth's people still clutch the rags of their own hopes about them, huddling in the chinked hovels of cultures and states numb in the biting winds of horror that blow across an earth unyielding as iron. We look about us at atrocity, prejudice, and violence, and have the feeling that the world grows old, can but repeat its ancient sins, can but add darkness to darkness.

Yet this is but the more reason that we must take up the psalm and let its gospel of judgment be heard. The bleak midwinter is not the final truth about the world. Human life can not be reduced to a biological process of the survival of the fittest. It is not some Spanglerian organism in which cultures grow, mature, and age to die. History is not an inexorable dialectic of materialism worked out through class struggle. It would be and is all these things apart from God. But the psalm sets against them the great contradiction of the child—the king whose appearance is the light that shines in great darkness.

Around a school in New Orleans, a vengeful mob chants its carol, "We hate niggers," and through them walks a disciple with his little girl, to go to school. In the Congo, demonic forces have been pushed into a vacuum left by the failure of white and black people—and in the maelstrom a handful of disciples, missionaries, go on with their work of healing, teaching, and converting. In China where tyranny has frozen a whole people in fear and inhumanity, the little hidden church gathers in secret to contemplate God's child, to keep alive the memory of what the human is like. There is the miracle into which the psalm invites us.

Then sing a new song: For the King has come to judge the world in righteousness! "Joy to the world!"

20

A Psalm for Thanksgiving

Psalm 100

This is the last chapel series before our national day of Thanksgiving on Thursday of next week. The significance of this sequence may be somewhat obscured for some of us by another—that these days are the prelude to the first quarterly examinations of this session. A few of us may be in no mood to give thanks just now. If that be the case, then we need to hear the Word in the One Hundredth Psalm. Here is Scripture's call to a response to God that will not wait for quieter and freer times. It insists that the many things that press in upon us as the responsibilities of our vocation are the very occasions for praising God. It reminds us how bereft we would be if one day we awoke and they were all taken from us. How should we then answer our God when our lives were empty of the many things he has given us to do in that he has called us.

This psalm moves in lines of measured beauty toward the climax of Thanksgiving, and in that way teaches us what thanksgiving is: the joyful answer of the whole person to the grace of God in giving us our vocation.

"Make a joyful noise to the LORD all the land"—such is the imperative that rings forth in the opening measure. In the old Israel, this psalm was a summons to those who lived in the promised land, to the people whose life was possible at all by the fulfillment of God's promise to the fathers. It bid them shout aloud—shout as did the conquering armies when the victory was won, applaud as did the assembled nation when the king strode into their midst. But this time the acclaim is for the Lord, the covenant God. God's is the victory and God's the honor. Swiftly the summons moves on, and we hear the call twice more. "Serve the LORD with gladness, Come into his presence with exaltation." Each line reiterates the elements of the first. The invocation of joy is intensified, for it is not a Sunday smile for the sake of being sociable to which these words refer. It is the gladness that wells up from the whole person. It is the exquisite merriment that falls upon those whose attention is focused on the ultimate Good from whence derive all the good things of human existence— for all here is centered in God. "Serve him"—that is, worship him with the singleness of truth that what is done in the sanctuary is a symbol of total life. "Come into his presence"—that is, move toward the sanctuary, the place that the Lord's gracious condescension appoints as a rendezvous where the eternal may be found in time. Come in a pilgrimage that tutors all of life to be a movement toward the God who is present in God's Word and church. This is no more and no less than a liturgical statement of the answer to our ultimate question, "What is the chief end of man?" (Westminster Shorter Catechism). This query is the quandary of philosophy at its best, and poor, broken, inchoate attempts to answer appear in the life of everyone. But for those for whom the heavens have broken open, so that all is seen in terms of covenant and Christ, here is the answer: "Man's chief end is to glorify God and enjoy him forever."

The imperatives of the first movement of Old Hundred are not ended. We heard yet a fourth, a final one that summarizes and defines those already spoken. "Know ye that the LORD is God indeed." But is this not strange? We are bid *to know*, commanded *to know*! It is one thing to be called to sing and worship and come; these are responses of the heart and will. But "Know?" This is a matter of the mind. We need not be commanded, only told. Why does not the psalm simply state the proposition that the covenant Lord is God, and give that as the reason for worship? So we usually misunderstand this line.

But when we do, we miss the relation of the fourth imperative to the previous three, and misunderstand what it is that we are summoned to do. The knowing with which the psalm is concerned is fealty to the Godship of the covenant Lord. This is the content of the knowing: "He made us and *his* we are, his people and the flock of his pasturing." The knowledge of the God who chooses a people that they may be God's people—knowing the God who takes us who were no people and makes us a chosen race, a royal priesthood, a holy nation—this knowledge can occur only in faith and obedience. That "the LORD is God" is not merely a theological proposition with which we reason, not mere information to garnish the desert of pious religion. It is a definition of our own life, or it is nothing. It is an obeyed understanding of who we are and what we are to do. It is the structure of our existence. It is true for us only in that we are constantly about the business of being God's people. That is why we are summoned to know, and when the psalm takes up the call to thanksgiving, it does so on the basis of this definition. The only possible thanksgiving to the covenant Lord is the practice of our vocation, the discipleship of belonging to God.

In the light of such a radical notion of thanksgiving our national and personal courtesy to our national and personal God would seem to leave something to be desired. It is a nice custom that we have in late November. The president issues a proclamation, and a nation whose religion is more and more a matter of self-congratulation goes through the motions of gratitude. Governors and mayors say appropriate things. Preachers offer prayers before the few who can spare the time from football and hunting. Better this than nothing. Let us count our blessings, sneak a glance heavenward, and thank the nice God who gives us things. After all, we are what John Galbraith has called the "Affluent Society." Our current embarrassment is not material poverty, but a gross national product that outruns consumer demand. We are the first society in history that has had to create need. To quote him at one point: "To create the demand for automobiles we must contrive elaborate and functionless changes each year and then subject the consumer to ruthless psychological pressures to persuade him of their importance. Were this process to falter or break down, the consequences would be disturbing."

Disturbing indeed! But what ought to disturb the church in this affluent society is that it has done so little to invest this prosperity with a sense of vocation. Is it not our responsibility that we are a nation glutted with products and relatively poor in services? Have we no word for this society but "Say thank you to the nice God"? Perhaps we fail because we in the church have settled for things instead of vocation. Perhaps instead of redeeming a secular disposition to be grateful, we have accepted a secular definition of thanksgiving. Perhaps that is why an affluent church can raise more and more money and find it more and more difficult to plan effective and honest service to the King and his kingdom. Examine the postwar relationship between budgets for building expensive churches and budgets for missions, and think upon these things. Disturbing indeed!

And what of us? How carefully we go about separating the hard work of mastering exegesis and learning to think theologically from the things for which we are willing to say, "Thank you." We still reckon up our blessings just as we were taught in Sunday school, grudgingly ponder what we have, and stop short of remembering who we are. Too seldom does it occur to us that the sweat of learning the history of the church, the bother of studying to pastor people, the seemingly trivial details of a Sunday school lesson are the very stuff of our call—the hard, real, inescapable opportunity to be thankful. These things are the grace of God that frees us for thanksgiving.

Then, precisely in this week when more lies to hand than ever can be done, let us be thankful and receive it all as the gift of our vocation.

> Let us here and now make a joyful noise to our LORD
> > Serve him with gladness
> > Come into his presence with exaltation.
> Let us know by the very energy of our obedience that the
> > covenant LORD is God indeed,
> > > know through being his people, the flock of his pasturing.

21

Language for Lent

Psalm 142

This psalm is an entreaty to God to save, but there is not a word about sin in it. That makes it an enigma to all who think sin and salvation go exclusively together.

The psalm is clearly a confession of the human condition, but the theme and mood of penitence are never voiced. That makes it an anomaly in this season of Lent.

The psalm is a public cry of weakness and isolation, of simple personal desperation. That makes it an embarrassment to our canons of competence and sociability.

Psalm 142 is, of course, no oddity. It is only one of a larger number of similar prayers in the Psalter. There are more of them than psalms that make sin the subject of confession. In the Old Testament the poetry of human desperation is broader and larger and louder than poetry of penitence; indeed, it includes the latter within it as one important way, but only one way in which people stand in need of prayer and salvation.

The apparent anomaly of Psalm 142 read as Lenten text and prayer poses the question set by this whole liturgy of human desperation. What does this way of presenting the human condition to God have to do with our relation to the Paschal event of Jesus' death and resurrection? We are accustomed to the penitential psalms and think we know how to use them as confession of sin. What wisdom is there in the canon of Scripture and liturgical practice that gives us these confessions of finitude and mortality as language to help our silence before the Paschal event?

I wonder if prayers like Psalm 142 do not help us discern the human condition into which Jesus entered in his Passion. One of the fondest and firmest doctrines of the Christian faith is the full humanity of Jesus. Reflection on that doctrine has always been especially occupied with his suffering and death. In

183

liturgy, in creeds, in doctrine the church has sought to express and confess his humanity. But there is no place in the repertoire of available resources where the depths and misery, the vicissitudes and vulnerability, the precariousness of the human condition is expressed in such range and openness as in the psalms.

The New Testament prompts this use of the psalms. The connection between them and the Gospel narratives about Jesus are many. He began one of these psalms as his dying prayer: "*Eli, eli lama sabachthani?*" His words in Gethsemane echo their deepest note: "My soul is very sorrowful, even to death" (Mark 14:34). Where else are there prayers adequate for "and being in agony he prayed more earnestly; and his sweat became like great drops of blood falling upon the ground" (Luke 22:44)?

I do not think we can rely on our experience, our self-consciousness, our language to grasp what his passion, his identification with the human predicament, involves. We are too petty in our complaints, too limited in our empathies, too inhibited in our language; we will always trivialize. But these psalms do not trivialize. They may seem, rather, one vast exaggeration—until read toward his life. When we ask with Gerhard's great hymn on the Passion, "What language shall I borrow to thank thee, dearest friend, for this thy dying sorrow?" can there be any other answer than these psalms?

I wonder if we could not use this poetry of human desperation to discern our true and authentic neediness, to uncover how much is at issue for us in the Paschal event. The worshiping church has always known in its better wisdom what the answer is to the question "Who is it that prays in these prayers?"— has always known that it is the believer, individually and corporately, who holds this confession of mortality up to God. It is difficult to approach the celebration of Holy Week with anything like the sense of need and hope that would match its passionate drama, unless we are taught again and again to acknowledge the truth about ourselves. For ages believers have taken up these prayers, tried them on, rehearsed them in the musing of devotion and the chanting of liturgies, have come to themselves through these words—and silently known, "This is who—what I am."

We need the help of these prayers, because in our culture there are forces that conspire to deny the wisdom of looking clearly at our finitude. Materialism distracts attention from the human dimensions of existence. The medicines of technology ease the symptoms of our mortality. Our culture is still gripped with an orthodoxy of competence and happiness, however sorely tried that orthodoxy is today. In all this our time and place may not be so different from that of the psalms. Thinkers from Father Athanasius to Ernest Becker have tried to show us that, at bottom, human culture is a conspiracy to subvert death. And in the usual liturgy of the church, the notion is nurtured that the confession of sin completes the agenda of presenting our need for salvation.

The exposure of our need is completed in the recitation of what we have done that we ought not to have done—as though what has been done to us, and what is happening to us, and what we cannot do—as though all this does not count in the neediness we bring to the Paschal event. Thinkers from Father Athanasius to Ernest Becker have tried to show us that human evil itself arises from the attempt to deal with our finitude.

These prayers open us up to the depth and ultimacy of our need for salvation, the salvation given through the crucified and risen Jesus. They make us ready to rehearse with him in his Passion the only way to enact our finitude as creatures whose bodies are a process of nature and whose destiny is a part of history. They quicken the thirst in us for the living Spirit, his Spirit, which is received and experienced as an anticipation of our own resurrection.

> Let us pray:
> Crucified and risen Lord—
> You are our only true security
> You are all we can be sure of in life and death.
> Free us from the power of evil and death
>   to which our fears and weaknesses make us captive.
> Liberate us—to praise you with lives of trust and hope
> And now
>   May the present mercy of God
>   accompany you on the way
>   and fill our lives with peace.

Notes

Chapter 4

1. For an overview of the "laments of an individual" and the companion genres, see, among others, Claus Westermann, *Praise and Lament in the Psalms* (Atlanta: John Knox Press, 1981).
2. The use of the term "self" in this way is not intended to introduce the complex discussion in psychology and philosophy about the nature and relationship of self, ego, person, etc. See, for instance, chaps. 4–6 in Wolfhart Pannenberg, *Anthropology in Theological Perspective* (Philadelphia: Westminster Press, 1985).
3. On the identification of the user with the self in the psalms see chap. 5 in James L. Mays, *The Lord Reigns: A Theological Handbook to the Psalms* (Louisville, KY: Westminster John Knox Press, 1994).
4. For an extensive account of the typical elements that compose the prayers for help, see Patrick D. Miller, *They Cried to the Lord* (Minneapolis: Fortress Press, 1994), chap. 3.
5. See the exposition of Psalm 13 in Mays, *The Lord Reigns*, 55ff.
6. Examples of lament-prayers from the ancient Near East are collected in J. B. Pritchard, *Ancient Near Eastern Texts Relating to the Old Testament* (Princeton, NJ: Princeton University Press, 1969).
7. The complexity of the self in the prayers is discussed in Mays, *The Lord Reigns*, 40–45
8. On the "anthropology" of Psalm 8, see James L. Mays, "What Is a Human Being? Reflections on Psalm 8," *Theology Today* 50, no. 4 (January 1994): 511–20 (see pp. 97–106 of this volume).
9. On "image of God" and its importance in theological anthropology see R. Kendall Soulen and Linda Woodhead, eds. *God and Human Dignity* (New York: T. & T. Clark, 2005, [forthcoming]).
10. On *ṣelem* and *demut* in the Old Testament, see E. Jenni and C. Westermann, eds., *Theologisches Handwoerterbuch zum Alten Testament*, vol. 2 (Munich: Chr. Kaiser Verlag, 1976), cols. 556–63.
11. The *Sitz-im-Leben* of the plural style is identified in Patrick D. Miller, *Genesis 1–11: Studies in Structure and Theme*, Journal for the Study of the Old Testament, Supplement Series 8 (Sheffield: University of Sheffield, 1978), 9–26.

12. On the phrase "knowing/knowledge of good and evil," see Jenni and Wester-mann, *Theologisches*, vol. 1, cols. 687–91.
13. See "In a Vision: the Portrayal of the Messiah in the Psalms," in Mays, *The Lord Reigns*, 99ff.
14. On the prayers for help as used in the passion narrative of the Gospels, see James L. Mays, "Prayer and Christology: Psalm 22 as Perspective on the Passion," *Theology Today* 42, no. 3 (October 1985): 322ff.
15. On the importance of this saying for Christology see James L. Mays, "Now I Know: An Exposition of Genesis 22:1–19 and Matthew 26:36–46" in *Theology Today*, 58, no. 4 (January 2004), 519–25.
16. On "image of God" in Pauline letters, see Udo Schnelle, *The Human Condition: Anthropology in the Teachings of Jesus, Paul and John* (Minneapolis: Fortress Press, 1996), 98–102.
17. Westminster Shorter Catechism, q. 1.
18. *Against Heresies* 4.20.7.

Chapter 6

1. G. Wilson, *The Editing of the Hebrew Psalter*, Society of Biblical Literature Dissertation Series 76 (Chico, CA: Scholars Press, 1985); "Evidence of Editorial Divisions in the Hebrew Psalter," *Vetus Testamentum* 34 (1984): 337–52; "The Use of 'Untitled' Psalms in the Hebrew Psalter," *Zeitschrift für die alttestamentliche Wissenschaft* 97 (1985): 404–13; "The Use of Royal Psalms at the 'Seams' of the Hebrew Psalter," *Journal for the Study of the Old Testament* 35 (1986): 85–94.
2. J. Becker, *Israel deutet seine Psalmen: Urform and Neuinterpretation in den Psalmen*, Stuttgarter Bibelstudien 18 (Stuttgart: Katholisches Bibelwerk, 1966).
3. F. Stolz, *Psalmen im nachkultischen Raum*, Theologische Studien 129 (Zurich: Theologishen Verlag, 1983).
4. T. Veijola, *Verheissung in der Krise: Studien zur Literatur und Theologie der Exilszeit anhand des 89 Psalms* (Helsinki: Suomalainen Tiedeakatemia, 1982); W. Beyerlin, *Werden und Wesen des 107 Psalms*, Beihefte zur Zeitschrift für die alttestamentliche Wissenchaft 153 (Berlin: W. de Gruter, 1978).
5. B. S. Childs, *Introduction to the Old Testament as Scripture* (Philadelphia: Fortress Press, 1979); K. Seybold, *Introducing the Psalms*, trans. R. G. Dunphy (Edinburgh: T. & T. Clark, 1990).
6. J. L. Mays, "The Place of the Torah-Psalms in the Psalter," *Journal of Biblical Literature* 106, no. 1 (1987): 3–12.

Chapter 7

1. The quotations in this paper (and page numbers cited) are taken from the first volume of the translation published by the Calvin Translation Society, *Commentary on the Book of Psalms by John Calvin*, trans. James Anderson (Edinburgh, 1845). A revision of the translation by Arthur Golding (1571) has been undertaken by T. H. L. Parker, but only one volume has appeared: *A Commentary on the Psalms by John Calvin*, vol. 1 (London: James Clark and Co., 1965).
2. For information about the writing of the commentary, see, among others, T. H. L. Parker, *Calvin's Old Testament Commentaries* (Edinburgh: T. & T. Clark, 1986), 26–31; and also Parker's introduction to the volume listed in n. 1.
3. See the observations by Parker on page 12 of his introduction to the volume listed in n. 1.

Chapter 13

1. In addition to his published works on Deuteronomy and the psalms, see especially Miller's presidential address to the Society of Biblical Literature: "Deuteronomy and Psalms: Evoking a Biblical Conversation," *Journal of Biblical Literature* 118 (Spring 1999): 3–18.
2. The translation is my own.
3. Note the assumption behind the language of Pss. 23:5; 92:10; 141:5; and Luke 7:46.
4. Gen. 13:6 ("they, [Abram and Lot], could not dwell together") and 36:7 ("their [Esau's and Jacob's] possessions were too great for them to dwell together") illustrate the social arrangement and its problems.
5. E. Jenni, "אח *'ah* brother," *Theological Lexicon of the Old Testament*, ed. E. Jenni and C. Westermann (Peabody, MA: Hendrickson, 1997), 1:73–77, esp. 76–77.
6. E.g., Pss. 16:11; 21:4; 36:9.
7. Deut. 28:8; cf. Lev. 25:21.
8. Deut. 30:15–20.
9. G. Gerleman, "חיה *hyh*, to live," *Theological Lexicon of the Old Testament*, 1:417.
10. Quoted in J. J. Stewart Perowne, *The Book of Psalms*, 2 vols. (Andover, MA: Warren F. Draper, 1898), 2:395.